interchange
FOURTH EDITION

Jack C. Richards

With Jonathan Hull and Susan Proctor

Series Editor: David Bohlke

CAMBRIDGE
UNIVERSITY PRESS

STUDENT'S BOOK **2B**

CAMBRIDGE
UNIVERSITY PRESS

32 Avenue of the Americas, New York, NY 10013-2473, USA

Cambridge University Press is part of the University of Cambridge.

It furthers the University's mission by disseminating knowledge in the pursuit of education, learning and research at the highest international levels of excellence.

www.cambridge.org
Information on this title: www.cambridge.org/9781107650923

First published 2006
7th printing 2014

Printed in Mexico by Quad/ Graphics Queretaro, S.A. de C.V.

A catalog record for this publication is available from the British Library.

ISBN 978-1-107-64869-2 Student's Book 2 with Self-study DVD-ROM
ISBN 978-1-107-64410-6 Student's Book 2A with Self-study DVD-ROM
ISBN 978-1-107-62676-8 Student's Book 2B with Self-study DVD-ROM
ISBN 978-1-107-64873-9 Workbook 2
ISBN 978-1-107-61698-1 Workbook 2A
ISBN 978-1-107-65075-6 Workbook 2B
ISBN 978-1-107-62527-3 Teacher's Edition 2 with Assessment Audio CD/CD-ROM
ISBN 978-1-107-62941-7 Class Audio 2 CDs
ISBN 978-1-107-62500-6 Full Contact 2 with Self-study DVD-ROM
ISBN 978-1-107-63719-1 Full Contact 2A with Self-study DVD-ROM
ISBN 978-1-107-65092-3 Full Contact 2B with Self-study DVD-ROM

For a full list of components, visit www.cambridge.org/interchange

Art direction, book design, layout services, and photo research: Integra
Audio production: CityVox, NYC
Video production: Nesson Media Boston, Inc.

Welcome to *Interchange Fourth Edition*, the world's most successful English series!

Interchange offers a complete set of tools for learning how to communicate in English.

Student's Book
with **NEW Self-study DVD-ROM**

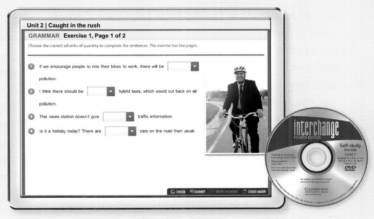

- **Complete video program** with additional **video exercises**

- Additional **vocabulary**, **grammar**, **speaking**, **listening**, and **reading** practice
- Printable **score reports** to submit to teachers

Available online

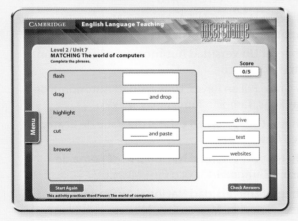

Interchange Arcade

- **Free** self-study website
- **Fun**, interactive, self-scoring activities
- Practice **vocabulary**, **grammar**, **listening**, and **reading**
- **MP3s** of the class audio program

Online Workbook

- A variety of **interactive activities** that correspond to each Student's Book lesson
- **Instant feedback** for hundreds of activities
- **Easy to use** with clear, easy-to-follow instructions
- Extra **listening practice**
- Simple tools for teachers to **monitor progress** such as scores, attendance, and time spent online

Authors' acknowledgments

A great number of people contributed to the development of *Interchange Fourth Edition*. Particular thanks are owed to the reviewers using *Interchange, Third Edition* in the following schools and institutes – their insights and suggestions have helped define the content and format of the fourth edition:

Ian Geoffrey Hanley, **The Address Education Center**, Izmir, Turkey

James McBride, **AUA Language Center**, Bangkok, Thailand

Jane Merivale, **Centennial College**, Toronto, Ontario, Canada

Elva Elena Peña Andrade, **Centro de Auto Aprendizaje de Idiomas**, Nuevo León, Mexico

José Paredes, **Centro de Educación Continua de la Escuela Politécnica Nacional** (CEC-EPN), Quito, Ecuador

Chia-jung Tsai, **Changhua University of Education**, Changhua City, Taiwan

Kevin Liang, **Chinese Culture University**, Taipei, Taiwan

Roger Alberto Neira Perez, **Colegio Santo Tomás de Aquino**, Bogotá, Colombia

Teachers at **Escuela Miguel F. Martínez**, Monterrey, Mexico

Maria Virgínia Goulart Borges de Lebron, **Great Idiomas**, São Paulo, Brazil

Gina Kim, **Hoseo University**, Chungnam, South Korea

Heeyong Kim, Seoul, South Korea

Elisa Borges, **IBEU-Rio**, Rio de Janeiro, Brazil

Jason M. Ham, **Inha University**, Incheon, South Korea

Rita de Cássia S. Silva Miranda, **Instituto Batista de Idiomas**, Belo Horizonte, Brazil

Teachers at **Instituto Politécnico Nacional**, Mexico City, Mexico

Victoria M. Roberts and Regina Marie Williams, **Interactive College of Technology**, Chamblee, Georgia, USA

Teachers at **Internacional de Idiomas**, Mexico City, Mexico

Marcelo Serafim Godinho, **Life Idiomas**, São Paulo, Brazil

J. Kevin Varden, **Meiji Gakuin University**, Yokohama, Japan

Rosa Maria Valencia Rodríguez, Mexico City, Mexico

Chung-Ju Fan, **National Kinmen Institute of Technology**, Kinmen, Taiwan

Shawn Beasom, **Nihon Daigaku**, Tokyo, Japan

Gregory Hadley, **Niigata University of International and Information Studies**, Niigata, Japan

Chris Ruddenklau, **Osaka University of Economics and Law**, Osaka, Japan

Byron Roberts, **Our Lady of Providence Girls' High School**, Xindian City, Taiwan

Simon Banha, **Phil Young's English School**, Curitiba, Brazil

Flávia Gonçalves Carneiro Braathen, **Real English Center**, Viçosa, Brazil

Márcia Cristina Barboza de Miranda, **SENAC**, Recife, Brazil

Raymond Stone, **Seneca College of Applied Arts and Technology**, Toronto, Ontario, Canada

Gen Murai, **Takushoku University**, Tokyo, Japan

Teachers at **Tecnológico de Estudios Superiores de Ecatepec**, Mexico City, Mexico

Teachers at **Universidad Autónoma Metropolitana–Azcapotzalco**, Mexico City, Mexico

Teachers at **Universidad Autónoma de Nuevo León**, Monterrey, Mexico

Mary Grace Killian Reyes, **Universidad Autónoma de Tamaulipas**, Tampico Tamaulipas, Mexico

Teachers at **Universidad Estatal del Valle de Ecatepec**, Mexico City, Mexico

Teachers at **Universidad Nacional Autónoma de Mexico – Zaragoza**, Mexico City, Mexico

Teachers at **Universidad Nacional Autónoma de Mexico – Iztacala**, Mexico City, Mexico

Luz Edith Herrera Diaz, Veracruz, Mexico

Seri Park, **YBM PLS**, Seoul, South Korea

Self-assessment charts revised by Alex Tilbury
Grammar plus written by Karen Davy

Plan of Book 2B

Titles/Topics	Speaking	Grammar
UNIT 9 PAGES 58–63		
Times have changed! Life in the past, present, and future; changes and contrasts; consequences	Talking about change; comparing time periods; describing possible consequences	Time contrasts; conditional sentences with *if* clauses
UNIT 10 PAGES 64–69		
I hate working on weekends. Abilities and skills; job preferences; personality traits; careers	Describing abilities and skills; talking about job preferences; describing personality traits	Gerunds; short responses; clauses with *because*
PROGRESS CHECK PAGES 70–71		
UNIT 11 PAGES 72–77		
It's really worth seeing! Landmarks and monuments; world knowledge	Talking about landmarks and monuments; describing countries; discussing facts	Passive with *by* (simple past); passive without *by* (simple present)
UNIT 12 PAGES 78–83		
What happened? Storytelling; unexpected recent past events	Describing recent past events and experiences; discussing someone's activities lately	Past continuous vs. simple past; present perfect continuous
PROGRESS CHECK PAGES 84–85		
UNIT 13 PAGES 86–91		
Good book, terrible movie! Entertainment; movies and books; reactions and opinions	Describing movies and books; talking about actors and actresses; asking for and giving reactions and opinions	Participles as adjectives; relative pronouns for people and things
UNIT 14 PAGES 92–97		
So that's what it means! Nonverbal communication; gestures and meaning; signs; drawing conclusions	Interpreting body language; explaining gestures and meanings; describing acceptable and prohibited behavior in different situations; asking about signs and their meaning	Modals and adverbs: *might, may, could, must, maybe, perhaps, possibly, probably, definitely*; permission, obligation, and prohibition
PROGRESS CHECK PAGES 98–99		
UNIT 15 PAGES 100–105		
What would you do? Money; hopes; predicaments; speculations	Speculating about past and future events; describing a predicament; giving advice and suggestions	Unreal conditional sentences with *if* clauses; past modals
UNIT 16 PAGES 106–111		
What's your excuse? Requests; excuses; invitations	Reporting what people said; making polite requests; making invitations and excuses	Reported speech: requests and statements
PROGRESS CHECK PAGES 112–113		
GRAMMAR PLUS PAGES 140–147, 150–151		

Pronunciation/Listening	Writing/Reading	Interchange Activity
Intonation in statements with time phrases Listening to people talk about changes	Writing a paragraph describing a person's past, present, and possible future "Are you in love?": Reading about the signs of being in love	"Consider the consequences": Agreeing and disagreeing with classmates
Unreleased and released /t/ and /d/ Listening to people talk about their job preferences	Writing a cover letter for a job application "Find the Job That's Right for You!": Reading about how personality type affects career choices	"Dream job": Interviewing for a job
The letter o Listening to descriptions of monuments; listening for information about a country	Writing a guidebook introduction "A Guide to Unusual Museums": Reading about interesting museums	"Who is this by?": Sharing information about famous works
Contrastive stress in responses Listening to stories about unexpected experiences	Writing a description of a recent experience "From the Streets to the Screen": Reading about the rise of an unusual group of musicians	"Life is like a game!": Playing a board game to share past experiences
Emphatic stress Listening for opinions; listening to a movie review	Writing a movie review "Special Effects": Reading about the history of special effects	"Famous faces": Asking classmates' opinions about movies, TV shows, and celebrities
Pitch Listening to people talk about the meaning of signs	Writing a list of rules "Pearls of Wisdom": Reading about proverbs and their meaning	"What's going on?": Interpreting body language
Reduction of have Listening to people talk about predicaments; listening to a call-in radio show	Writing a letter to an advice columnist "The Advice Circle": Reading an online advice forum	"Do the right thing!": Deciding what to do in a difficult situation
Reduction of had and would Listening for excuses	Writing a report about people's responses to a survey; "The Truth About Lying": Reading about "white lies"	"Excuses, excuses": Discussing calendar conflicts and making up excuses

Times have changed!

1 SNAPSHOT

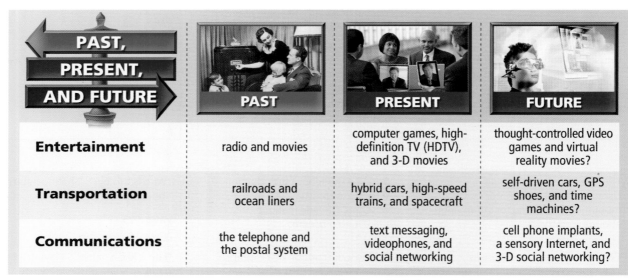

PAST, PRESENT, AND FUTURE	PAST	PRESENT	FUTURE
Entertainment	radio and movies	computer games, high-definition TV (HDTV), and 3-D movies	thought-controlled video games and virtual reality movies?
Transportation	railroads and ocean liners	hybrid cars, high-speed trains, and spacecraft	self-driven cars, GPS shoes, and time machines?
Communications	the telephone and the postal system	text messaging, videophones, and social networking	cell phone implants, a sensory Internet, and 3-D social networking?

Sources: www.futureforall.org; www.inventors.about.com; http://toptrends.nowandnext.com

Which of these past and present developments are the most important? Why?
Do you think any of the future developments could happen in your lifetime?
Can you think of two other developments that could happen in the future?

2 CONVERSATION *That's progress!*

A ▶ Listen and practice.

Tanya: This neighborhood sure has changed!

Matt: I know. A few years ago, not many people lived here. But the population is growing so fast these days.

Tanya: Remember how we used to rent videotapes at that little video store?

Matt: Yeah. Now it's a multiplex cinema.

Tanya: And I hear they're tearing down our high school. They're going to build a shopping mall. Soon, there will be just malls and parking lots.

Matt: That's because everyone has a car! Fifty years ago, people walked everywhere. Nowadays, they drive.

Tanya: That's progress, I guess.

B ▶ Listen to the rest of the conversation.
What else has changed in their neighborhood?

3 GRAMMAR FOCUS

Time contrasts ▶

Past	Present	Future
A few years ago, not many people **lived** here.	These days, the population **is growing** so fast.	Soon, there **will be** apartment blocks everywhere.
People **used to rent** videotapes.	Today, people **download** movies online.	In a few years, movie theaters **might not exist**.
Fifty years ago, people **walked** everywhere.	Nowadays, people **drive** their cars instead.	People **are going to have** self-driven cars in the future.

A Complete the sentences in column A with the appropriate information from column B. Then compare with a partner.

A

1. About 60 years ago, ...h....
2. Before the automobile, ...
3. Before there were supermarkets, ...
4. In most offices these days, ...
5. In many cities nowadays, ...
6. In many classrooms today, ...
7. In the next 100 years, ...
8. Sometime in the near future, ...

B

a. people used to shop at small grocery stores.
b. pollution is becoming a serious problem.
c. students are learning with interactive whiteboards.
d. people didn't travel as much from city to city.
e. there will probably be cities in space.
f. people work more than 40 hours a week.
g. doctors might find a cure for the common cold.
h. many TV shows were in black and white.

B Complete four of the phrases in part A, column A, with your own ideas. Then compare with a partner.

4 PRONUNCIATION *Intonation in statements with time phrases*

A ▶ Listen and practice. Notice the intonation in these statements beginning with a time phrase.

In the past, very few people used computers.

Today, people use computers all the time.

In the future, there will be a computer in every home.

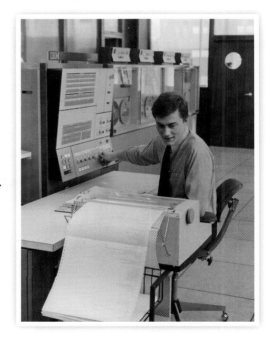

B PAIR WORK Complete these statements with your own information. Then read your statements to a partner. Pay attention to intonation.

As a child, I used to . . .	These days, . . .
Five years ago, I . . .	In five years, I'll . . .
Nowadays, I . . .	In ten years, I might . . .

5 LISTENING *For better or for worse*

A Listen to people discuss changes. Check (✓) the topic each person talks about.

Topic		Change		Better or worse?	
1. ☐ population	☐ environment	....		☐	☐
2. ☐ transportation	☐ cities	....		☐	☐
3. ☐ families	☐ shopping	....		☐	☐

B Listen again. Write down the change and check (✓) if things are better or worse now.

6 SPEAKING *Changing times*

GROUP WORK How have things changed? How will things be different in the future? Choose four of these topics. Then discuss the questions below.

education   fashion   shopping
entertainment   food   sports
environment   housing   technology

What was it like in the past?
What is it like today?
What will it be like in the future?

A: In the past, people listened to sports on the radio.
B: Nowadays, they can watch sports on HDTVs , too.
C: In the future, . . .

7 WRITING *A description of a person*

A **PAIR WORK** Interview your partner about his or her past, present, and hopes for the future.

B Write a paragraph describing how your partner has changed. Make some predictions about the future. Don't write your partner's name.

> This person moved to our school several years ago. She used to be the quietest girl in the class. Now, she's in the drama club and loves to watch soap operas. Someday, she'll be a successful actress. She'll be famous. She'll star in movies and on TV. I think she'll . . .

C **CLASS ACTIVITY** Read your paragraph to the class. Can they guess who it is about?

8 PERSPECTIVES *Take the good with the bad.*

A Listen to some possible consequences of getting a high-paying job. Check (✓) the statements you agree with.

If you get a high-paying job, ...

.... you'll have more cash to spend.
.... you'll be able to buy anything you want.
.... you'll be able to travel first class.
.... you might have to pay higher taxes.
.... you'll be able to donate more to charities.
.... more people may want to be your friend.
.... you may get your own office.
.... you won't have as much stress in your life.
.... people will ask you for a loan.
.... you'll have a lot more free time.

B PAIR WORK Look at the statements again. Which are advantages of getting a high-paying job? Which are disadvantages?

"The first one is an advantage. Everyone would like to have more money!"

9 GRAMMAR FOCUS

Conditional sentences with if clauses ▶

Possible situation (present)	Consequence (future with will, may, or might)
If you **get** a high-paying job,	you**'ll have** more cash to spend.
If you **have** more cash to spend,	you**'ll be able to buy** anything you want.
If you **can buy** anything you want,	you **won't save** your money.
If you **don't save** your money,	you **may need** another job.

A Match the *if* clauses in column A with the appropriate consequences from column B. Then compare with a partner.

A
1. If you eat less sugar, ...
2. If you walk to work every day, ...
3. If you don't get enough sleep, ...
4. If you change jobs, ...
5. If you don't get married, ...
6. If you travel abroad, ...

B
a. you'll be able to experience a new culture.
b. you might feel a lot healthier.
c. you'll stay in shape without joining a gym.
d. you'll have more money to spend on yourself.
e. you won't be able to stay awake in class.
f. you may not like it better than your old one.

B Add your own consequences to the *if* clauses in column A. Then practice with a partner.

"If you eat less sugar, you'll lose weight."

10 WORD POWER Consequences

A PAIR WORK Can you find two consequences for each possible situation?
Complete the chart with information from the list.

communicate in a different language
earn your own spending money
experience culture shock
feel jealous sometimes
get in shape
get into a good college
get married
get valuable work experience
improve your grades
pay membership dues

Possible situation	Consequences
fall in love	....
get a part-time job	....
join a gym	....
move to a foreign country	....
study very hard	....

B GROUP WORK Share your answers with the group. Can you think of
one more consequence for each event?

11 SPEAKING Unexpected consequences

A GROUP WORK Choose three possible events from Exercise 10.
One student completes an event with a consequence. The next
student adds a consequence. Suggest at least five consequences.

A: If you study very hard, you'll improve your grades.
B: If you improve your grades, you'll get into a good school.
C: If you get into a good school, you may get a good job.
D: If you get a good job, you'll make a lot of money.
A: If you make a lot of money, you may have more stress.

B CLASS ACTIVITY Who has the most interesting consequences for each event?

12 INTERCHANGE 9 Consider the consequences

Give your opinion about some issues. Go to Interchange 9 on page 123.

Are you in LOVE?

What is the difference between "having a crush" on someone and falling in love?

You think you're falling in love. You're really attracted to a certain person. But this has happened before, and it was just a "crush." How can you tell if it's real this time? Here's what our readers said:

If you're falling in love, . . .

♥ you'll find yourself talking to, calling, or texting the person for no reason. (You might pretend there's a reason, but often there's not.)

♥ you'll find yourself bringing this person into every conversation. ("When I was in Mexico – ," a friend begins. You interrupt with, "My boyfriend made a great Mexican dinner last week.")

♥ you might suddenly be interested in things you used to avoid. ("When a woman asks me to tell her all about football, I know she's fallen in love," said a TV sports announcer.)

OK, so you've fallen in love. But falling in love is one thing, and staying in love is another. How can you tell, as time passes, that you're still in love?

If you stay in love, your relationship will change. You might not talk as much about the person you are in love with. You might not call him or her so often. But this person will nevertheless become more and more important in your life.

You'll find that you can be yourself with this person. When you first fell in love, you were probably afraid to admit certain things about yourself. But now you can be totally honest. You can trust him or her to accept you just as you are. Falling in love is great – staying in love is even better!

A Read the article. Where do you think it is from? Check (✓) the correct answer.

☐ an online news service ☐ a magazine ☐ an advice column ☐ an advertisement

B What things happen when you're falling in love compared with staying in love? Complete the chart.

Falling in love	Staying in love
1.	1. ....
2.	2. ....
3.	3. ....

C **PAIR WORK** Which do you think is more difficult – falling in love or staying in love? Can you think of other signs of being in love?

10 I hate working on weekends.

1 SNAPSHOT

EIGHT IMPORTANT JOB SKILLS
Here are some questions that employers might ask about your skills.

☐ 1. Can you **use a computer**?

☐ 2. Can you **manage other people**?

☐ 3. Are you **good at public speaking**?

☐ 4. Can you **teach others** how to do things?

☐ 5. Can you **solve problems**?

☐ 6. Do you **manage money well**?

☐ 7. Do you **work well with people**?

☐ 8. Do you **speak other languages**?

Source: U.S. Department of Labor

Which of these skills do you think are most important? Why?
Check (✓) the skills that you think you have.
Look at the skills you checked. What jobs do you think you might be good at?

2 CONVERSATION *I need a job!*

A ▶ Listen and practice.

Dan: I'm so broke. I really need to find a job!
Brad: So do I. Do you see anything good listed?
Dan: How about this telephone sales job? You call people and try to sell them magazines.
Brad: That sounds boring. And anyway, I'm not very good at selling.
Dan: Well, I am! I might check that one out. Oh, here's one for you. An assistant entertainment director on a cruise ship.
Brad: That sounds like fun. I love traveling, and I've never been on a cruise ship.
Dan: It says here you have to work every day while the ship is at sea.
Brad: That's OK. I don't mind working long hours if the pay is good. I think I'll apply for it.

B ▶ Listen to Brad's phone call. What else does the job require?

64

3 ## GRAMMAR FOCUS

Gerunds; short responses

Affirmative statements with gerunds	Agree	Disagree	Other verbs or phrases followed by gerunds
I love traveling.	So do I.	I don't.	
I hate working on weekends.	So do I.	Really? I like it.	like
I'm good at using a computer.	So am I.	Oh, I'm not.	enjoy
Negative statements with gerunds			be interested in
I don't mind working long hours.	Neither do I.	I do.	
I'm not good at selling.	Neither am I.	Well, I am.	
I can't stand commuting.	Neither can I.	Oh, I don't mind.	

A **PAIR WORK** Match the phrases in columns A and B to make statements about yourself. Then take turns reading your sentences and giving short responses.

A
1. I hate ....
2. I'm not very good at ....
3. I'm good at ....
4. I don't like ....
5. I can't stand ....
6. I'm interested in ....
7. I don't mind ....
8. I enjoy ....

B
a. talking on the phone.
b. working with a group or team.
c. solving other people's problems.
d. sitting in long meetings.
e. working on weekends.
f. eating lunch out every day.
g. managing my time.
h. learning foreign languages.

A: I hate working on weekends.
B: So do I.

B **GROUP WORK** Complete the phrases in column A with your own information. Then take turns reading your statements. Ask questions to get more information.

4 ## PRONUNCIATION *Unreleased and released* /t/ *and* /d/

A ▶ Listen and practice. Notice that when the sound /t/ or /d/ at the end of a word is followed by a consonant, it's unreleased. When it is followed by a vowel sound, it's released.

Unreleased
She's not good at math and science.

I hate working on Sundays.

You need to manage money well.

Released
He's not a good artist.

They really hate it!

I need a cup of coffee.

B **PAIR WORK** Write three sentences starting with *I'm not very good at* and *I don't mind*. Then practice the sentences. Pay attention to the unreleased and released sounds /t/ and /d/.

5 SPEAKING The right job

A **PAIR WORK** How does your partner feel about doing these things?
Interview your partner. Check (✓) his or her answers.

How do you feel about . . . ?	I enjoy it.	I don't mind it.	I hate it.
asking for help	☐	☐	☐
using a computer	☐	☐	☐
leading a team	☐	☐	☐
traveling	☐	☐	☐
creating spreadsheets	☐	☐	☐
talking on the phone	☐	☐	☐
working with people	☐	☐	☐
meeting deadlines	☐	☐	☐
working on the weekend	☐	☐	☐
managing money	☐	☐	☐
telling people what to do	☐	☐	☐
working with numbers	☐	☐	☐
public speaking	☐	☐	☐

B **PAIR WORK** Look back at the information in part A. Suggest a job for your partner.

"You enjoy creating spreadsheets and working with numbers. And you don't mind
managing money. I think you'd be a good accountant."

6 LISTENING Job hunting

A ◉ Listen to people talk about the kind of work they are looking for.
Check (✓) the job that would be best for each person.

1. Bill
   ☐ flight attendant
   ☐ teacher
   ☐ songwriter

2. Shannon
   ☐ lawyer
   ☐ bookkeeper
   ☐ doctor

3. Ben
   ☐ marine biologist
   ☐ model
   ☐ architect

B ◉ Listen again. Answer these questions.

1. What kind of job is Bill *not* interested in? ....
2. What is his attitude toward making money? ....
3. What do Shannon's family members do for a living? ....
4. What does she want to do before she gets a job? ....
5. What has Ben done to break into movies? ....
6. What does he show the interviewer? ....

7 INTERCHANGE 10 Dream job

Decide which job to apply for. Go to Interchange 10 on page 124.

WORD POWER *Personality traits*

A Which of these adjectives are positive (**P**)? Which are negative (**N**)?

creative	....P....	impatient	....
critical	....	level-headed	....
disorganized	....	moody	....
efficient	....	punctual	....
forgetful	....	reliable	....
generous	....	short-tempered	....
hardworking	....	strict	....

creative

impatient

B **PAIR WORK** Tell your partner about people you know with these personality traits.

"My neighbor is short-tempered. Sometimes he . . ."

C Listen to four conversations. Then check (✓) the adjective that best describes each person.

1. a boss
   - ☐ creative
   - ☐ forgetful
   - ☐ serious

2. a co-worker
   - ☐ unfriendly
   - ☐ generous
   - ☐ strange

3. a teacher
   - ☐ moody
   - ☐ patient
   - ☐ hardworking

4. a relative
   - ☐ short-tempered
   - ☐ disorganized
   - ☐ reliable

9 PERSPECTIVES *Job profiles*

A Listen to these people answer the question, "What kind of work would you like to do?" What job does each person talk about?

"Well, I think I'd make a good journalist because I'm good at writing. When I was in college, I worked as a reporter for the school website. I really enjoyed writing different kinds of articles."

"I know what I *don't* want to do! A lot of my friends work in the stock market, but I could never be a stockbroker because I can't make decisions quickly. I don't mind working hard, but I'm terrible under pressure!"

"I'm still in school. My parents want me to be a teacher, but I'm not sure yet. I guess I could be a teacher because I'm very creative. I'm also very impatient, so maybe I shouldn't work with kids."

B **PAIR WORK** Look at the interviews again. Who are you most like? least like? Why?

10 GRAMMAR FOCUS

> ## Clauses with because ▶
>
> *The word* because *introduces a cause or reason.*
>
> I'd make a good journalist **because I'm good at writing**.
> I could be a teacher **because I'm very creative**.
> I wouldn't want to be a teacher **because I'm very impatient**.
> I could never be a stockbroker **because I can't make decisions quickly**.

A Complete the sentences in column A with appropriate information from column B. Then compare with a partner.

A

1. I wouldn't want to be a nurse ....
2. I'd like to be a novelist ....
3. I could never be an accountant ....
4. I would make a bad waiter ....
5. I could be a flight attendant ....
6. I'd never work on a cruise ship ....

B

a. because I don't like hospitals.
b. because I really enjoy traveling.
c. because I have a terrible memory.
d. because I get seasick very easily.
e. because I love creative writing.
f. because I'm terrible with numbers.

B GROUP WORK Think about your personal qualities and skills. Then complete these statements. Take turns discussing them with your group.

I could never be a . . . because . . .
I wouldn't mind working as a . . . because . . .

I'd make a good . . . because . . .
The best job for me is . . . because . . .

11 WRITING *A cover letter for a job application*

A Imagine you are applying for one of the jobs in this unit. Write a short cover letter for a job application.

> Mr. Yoshioka
> Personnel Director
> Executive Airlines
>
> Dear Mr. Yoshioka,
>   I am responding to your recent advertisement in *The Post* for a bilingual international flight attendant. I think I'd make a good flight attendant for Executive Airlines because I'm a very friendly person and I really love traveling. I also enjoy meeting people.
>   As you can see from my résumé, I've had a lot of experience working with tourists. I worked at . . .

B PAIR WORK Exchange papers. If you received this letter, would you invite the applicant for a job interview? Why or why not?

Find the Job That's Right for You!

1 About half of all workers in the United States have jobs they aren't happy with. Don't let this happen to you! If you want to find the right job, don't rush to look through job ads on the Internet. Instead, sit down and think about yourself. What kind of person are you? What makes you happy?

2 According to psychologist John Holland, there are six types of personalities. Nobody is just one personality type, but most people are mainly one type. For each type, there are certain jobs that might be right and others that are probably wrong.

3 Considering your personality type can help you make the right job decision. Liz is a good example. Liz knew she wanted to do something for children. She thought she could help children as a school counselor or a lawyer. She took counseling and law courses – and hated them. After talking to a career counselor, she realized that she's an Artistic type. Liz studied film, and she now produces children's TV shows – and loves it.

Personality types

The Realistic type is practical and likes working with machines and tools.

The Investigative type is curious and likes to learn, analyze situations, and solve problems.

The Artistic type is imaginative and likes to express ideas by creating art.

The Social type is friendly and likes helping or training other people.

The Enterprising type is outgoing and likes to persuade or lead other people.

The Conventional type is careful and likes to follow routines and keep track of details.

A Read the article. Then find these sentences in the article. Is each sentence the main idea or a supporting idea in that paragraph? Check (✓) the correct boxes.

	Main idea	Supporting idea
1. About half of all workers . . . they aren't happy with. (par. 1)	☐	☐
2. According to psychologist . . . types of personalities. (par. 2)	☐	☐
3. For each type, there are . . . that are probably wrong. (par. 2)	☐	☐
4. Considering your personality . . . the right job decision. (par. 3)	☐	☐
5. After talking to a career counselor, . . . an Artistic type. (par. 3)	☐	☐

B For each personality type, write two examples of appropriate jobs. Then explain your answers to a partner.

Realistic	Investigative	Artistic	Social	Enterprising	Conventional
....	....	....	....	....	....
....	....	....	....	....	....

C **GROUP WORK** What personality type do you think you are? Does your group agree?

Units 9–10 Progress check

SELF-ASSESSMENT

How well can you do these things? Check (✓) the boxes.

I can	Very well	OK	A little
Describe people and things in the past, present, and future (Ex. 1)	☐	☐	☐
Describe possible consequences of actions (Ex. 2)	☐	☐	☐
Understand descriptions of abilities and personalities (Ex. 3, 4)	☐	☐	☐
Ask and answer questions about preferences and skills (Ex. 4)	☐	☐	☐
Give reasons for my opinions (Ex. 4)	☐	☐	☐

1 SPEAKING Past, present, and future

A PAIR WORK Think of one more question for each category. Then interview a partner.

Appearance   What did you use to look like? Can you describe yourself now?
What do you think you'll look like in the future?

Free time   Did you have a hobby as a child? What do you like to do these days?
How are you going to spend your free time next year?

B GROUP WORK Share one interesting thing about your partner.

2 GAME Truth and consequences

A Add two situations and two consequences to the lists below.

Situation	Consequence
☐ you move to a foreign country	☐ buy you a gift
☐ it's sunny tomorrow	☐ feel jealous sometimes
☐ it's cold tomorrow	☐ communicate in a new language
☐ you give me $10	☐ go to the beach
☐ you don't call me later	☐ get really angry
☐ you fall in love	☐ stay home
☐	☐ ....
☐	☐ ....

B CLASS ACTIVITY Go around the class and make sentences. Check (✓) each *if* clause
after you use it. The student who uses the most clauses correctly wins.

"If you move to a foreign country, you'll learn to . . ."

A ◉ Listen to Louisa and Tim discuss four jobs. Write down the jobs and check (✓) if they would be good or bad at them.

Job	Good	Bad	Reason
1. Louisa	☐	☐	....
....	☐	☐	....
2. Tim	☐	☐	....
....	☐	☐	....

B ◉ Listen again. What reasons do they give?

4 **DISCUSSION** *Job profile*

A Prepare a personal job profile. Write your name, skills, and job preferences. Think about the questions below. Then compare with a partner.

Are you good at . . . ?	**Do you . . . ?**	**Do you mind . . . ?**
communicating with people	have any special skills	traveling
solving problems	have any experience	working with a team
making decisions quickly	have a good memory	wearing a uniform
speaking foreign languages	manage money well	working long hours

A: Are you good at communicating with people?
B: Sure. I enjoy talking to people.
A: So do I. I like meeting new people and . . .

B GROUP WORK Make suggestions for possible jobs based on your classmates' job profiles. Give reasons for your opinions. What do you think of their suggestions for you?

A: Juan would be a good executive because he likes solving problems and making decisions quickly.
B: No way! I could never be an executive. I'm too disorganized!

WHAT'S NEXT?

Look at your Self-assessment again. Do you need to review anything?

11 It's really worth seeing!

1 SNAPSHOT

MODERN *Wonders*

The Lotus Temple in Delhi, India, was finished in 1986. Its lotus-shaped leaves are made of marble.

The Museum of Contemporary Art in Niterói, Brazil, is a modern, saucer-shaped structure.

The Millau Viaduct, over the Tam River in France, was opened in 2004. It's the tallest bridge in the world.

The National Stadium in Beijing, China, is also known as the Bird's Nest because of its unique appearance.

The Palm Islands of Dubai, U.A.E., were designed to look like palm trees. Construction was started in 2001.

Sources: http://science.discovery.com; www.thinkquest.org

Which of these wonders do you think is the most amazing? Why?
What other modern wonders do you know about? What are they? Where are they?
What modern wonders are in your country?

2 PERSPECTIVES *The Empire State Building*

A How much do you know about the Empire State Building?
Check (✓) the statements you think are true.

- ☐ 1. It was designed by an American architect.
- ☐ 2. It is in New York City.
- ☐ 3. It was officially opened by the president of the United States in 1931.
- ☐ 4. It took five years to build.
- ☐ 5. It cost $2 million to build.
- ☐ 6. There are 102 floors in the building.
- ☐ 7. There are colored lights at the top.
- ☐ 8. It is the tallest building in the world.

B ▶ Now listen and check your answers. What information is the most surprising?

3 GRAMMAR FOCUS

Passive with by (simple past) ▶

The passive changes the focus of a sentence.
For the simple past, use the past of be + past participle.

Active	**Passive**
The president **opened** the building in 1931.	It **was opened by** the president in 1931.
An American architect **designed** the building.	It **was designed by** an American architect.
In 1964, the building's owners **added** colored lights to the top.	Colored lights **were added** to the top **by** the building's owners in 1964.

A Complete the sentences with the simple past passive form of the verbs. Then compare with a partner.

1. The 2010 World Cup final .... (win) by Spain.
2. The film *Avatar* .... (direct) by James Cameron.
3. The novel *The Adventures of Huckleberry Finn* .... (write) by Mark Twain.
4. The songs "Revolution" and "Hey Jude" .... (record) by the Beatles in 1968.
5. *The Starry Night* .... (paint) by Vincent van Gogh.
6. The Shanghai Grand Theater .... (design) by French architect Jean-Marie Charpentier.
7. The opening ceremony of the 2012 London Olympics .... (see) by billions of people.
8. In the 2007 film *I'm Not There*, the American musician Bob Dylan .... (play) by six different people, including Australian actress Cate Blanchett.

B **PAIR WORK** Change these sentences into passive sentences with *by*. Then take turns reading them aloud.

1. Sculptor Frédéric-Auguste Bartholdi designed the Statue of Liberty in 1884.
....
2. Daniel Day-Lewis played Abraham Lincoln in the 2012 film *Lincoln*.
....
3. Gabriel García Márquez wrote the book *One Hundred Years of Solitude* in 1971.
....
4. Woo Paik produced the first digital HDTV in 1991.
....
5. J. K. Rowling wrote the first Harry Potter book on an old manual typewriter.
....
6. *Empire* magazine readers chose *The Godfather* as the greatest film of all time.
....

4 INTERCHANGE 11 *Who is this by?*

Who created these well-known works? Go to Interchange 11 on page 125.

It's really worth seeing! ■ 73

5 PRONUNCIATION *The letter o*

A ▶ Listen and practice. Notice how the letter *o* is pronounced in the following words.

/a/	/ou/	/u:/	/ʌ/
not	no	do	one
top	don't	food	love
....	....	....	....
....	....	....	....

B ▶ How is the letter *o* pronounced in these words? Write them in the correct column in part A. Then listen and check your answers.

come   done   lock   own   shot   soon   who   wrote

6 LISTENING *Who built them?*

▶ Listen to three tour guides describe some very old monuments.
Take notes to answer the questions below. Then compare with a partner.

the pyramids

Machu Picchu

the Great Wall of China

Who built them?   How big is the city?   Why was it built?
Why were they built?   When was it discovered?   How long is it?

7 WORD POWER *Local industry*

A Complete the chart. Then add one more word to each category.

cattle   oysters
✓ corn   sheep
electronics   shrimp
goats   soybeans
✓ lobsters   textiles
microchips   wheat

Farmed	Grown	Manufactured	Raised
lobsters	corn	....	....
....	....	....	....
....	....	....	....
....	....	....	....

B GROUP WORK Talk about things that are found in your country.

"We grow soybeans. We also manufacture cars."

8 CONVERSATION *I need some information.*

A ▶ Listen and practice.

Kelly: Hello?
John: Oh, hello. I need some information. What currency is used in the European Union?
Kelly: Where?
John: The European Union.
Kelly: I think the euro is used in most of Europe.
John: Oh, right. And is English spoken much there?
Kelly: I really have no idea.
John: Huh? Well, what about credit cards? Are they accepted everywhere?
Kelly: How would I know?
John: Well, you're a travel agent, aren't you?
Kelly: What? This is a hair salon. You have the wrong number!

B **PAIR WORK** Use information about a country you know to act out the conversation.

9 GRAMMAR FOCUS

Passive without by (simple present) ▶

For the simple present, use the present of **be** *+ past participle.*

Active	Passive
They **use** the euro in most of Europe.	The euro **is used** in most of Europe.
They **speak** English in many European countries.	English **is spoken** in many European countries.
They **manufacture** a lot of cars in Europe.	A lot of cars **are manufactured** in Europe.

A Complete this passage using the simple present passive form.

Many crops .... (grow) in Taiwan. Some crops .... (consume) locally, but others .... (export). Tea .... (grow) in cooler parts of the island, and rice .... (cultivate) in warmer parts. Fishing is also an important industry. A wide variety of seafood .... (catch) and .... (ship) all over the world. Many people .... (employ) in the electronics and textile industries as well.

B Complete the sentences. Use the passive of these verbs.

grow   make up   manufacture   raise   speak   use

1. French and English .... in Canada.
2. A lot of rice .... in Vietnam.
3. The U.S. .... of 50 states.
4. A lot of sheep .... in New Zealand.
5. Cars and computers .... in Korea.
6. The U.S. dollar .... in Ecuador.

C **PAIR WORK** Use the passive of the verbs in part B to talk about your country and other countries you know.

10 LISTENING Colombia

A ▶ Listen to a short talk about Colombia. Complete the chart.

Facts about Colombia	
Location	....
Population	....
Language	....
Industries	....
Agricultural products	....

Bogotá, Colombia

B ▶ Listen again. Check (✓) the things the speaker mentions about Colombia.

- ☐ beaches
- ☐ volcanoes
- ☐ snow-capped mountains
- ☐ rivers
- ☐ lakes
- ☐ hot lowland plains

11 SPEAKING Guess the country

A PAIR WORK Choose a country. Then answer these questions.

Where is it located?
What cities are found there?
What languages are spoken?

What currency is used?
What famous tourist attraction is found there?
What products are exported?

B CLASS ACTIVITY Give a short talk like the one in Exercise 10 about the country you chose. Don't say the country's name. Can the class guess the country?

12 WRITING A guidebook introduction

A Make an information chart like the one in Exercise 10 about a country you know. Then write an introduction for a guidebook about the country.

> Vietnam is located in Southeast Asia. It has a population of over 90 million people. Vietnamese is the official language. The country has many beautiful beaches, high mountains, and busy cities. Rice is grown in . . .

B GROUP WORK Exchange papers. Is any important information missing? Ask questions to find out more.

A Guide to Unusual Museums

Look at the pictures and scan the article. Where do you think you can see very old objects? a working factory? historic cooking tools?

1 Have you been to the Louvre in Paris, the National Museum of Anthropology in Mexico City, or any of those other "must see" museums? Well, now it's time to go off the beaten path.

The Kimchi Museum
Seoul, South Korea

2 If you don't know about kimchi, a trip to the Kimchi Museum is an eye-opening experience. The museum was founded in 1986 to highlight South Korea's rich kimchi culture. The exhibit includes displays of cooking utensils and materials related to making, storing, and eating the famous pickled vegetables. The museum also provides details about the history and nutritional benefits of South Korea's most beloved side dish. Finally, stop by the souvenir shop to try various types of kimchi.

The Museum of Gold
Bogotá, Colombia

3 If you want to see beautiful objects, the Museum of Gold is the place. It holds one of South America's most stunning collections. Because the exhibits sparkle so brightly, you can actually take photographs without using a flash on your camera! Not everything is made of gold, though. Among the exhibits are ancient pre-Columbian items. Many of them are made from a mixture of gold and copper, known as tumbaga.

The Chocolate Museum
Cologne, Germany

4 The Chocolate Museum will teach you everything about chocolate – from cocoa bean to candy bars. You'll learn about chocolate's 3,000-year history and discover how it was once used as money in South America. A real chocolate factory shows you how chocolate is made. After you've finished the tour, you can sample a complimentary drink of rich, gooey pure chocolate – perfect for those with a sweet tooth.

A Read the article. Find the words in *italics* below in the article. Then circle the meaning of each word or phrase.

1. When you *go off the beaten path*, you **do something unusual / go somewhere far away**.
2. When something is *founded*, it is **started / discovered**.
3. When something is *stunning*, it is extremely **attractive / large**.
4. When something is *ancient*, it is **very old / common**.
5. When something is *complimentary*, it is **free of charge / very expensive**.
6. When something is *gooey*, it is **light and refreshing / thick and sticky**.

B Where do these sentences belong? Write the number of the paragraph where each sentence could go.

.... a. Don't forget to buy your favorite kind to bring home for dinner!
.... b. Did you know that it wasn't popular in Europe until the nineteenth century?
.... c. The museum also features coins, jewelry, and pieces of rare art.
.... d. There are some museums that try to be a little different.

C **PAIR WORK** Which of these museums would you most like to visit? Why?

It's really worth seeing! ■ **77**

 What happened?

1 SNAPSHOT

 Where did the ideas for these *"accidental inventions"* come from?

The Popsicle

In 1905, 11-year-old Frank Epperson wanted to make a new soft drink. He mixed the ingredients with a stick, but he left the soda outside overnight. The next morning, he found it frozen with the stick inside.

Velcro

In 1948 George de Mestral went for a walk and noticed small seeds stuck to his clothes. He examined them under a microscope and found hundreds of small hooks that stuck to almost anything.

Post-it Notes

In 1970 Spencer Silver tried to invent a new glue, but it was very weak. No one wanted to use it. Four years later, his co-worker Arthur Fry put the glue on bookmarks to keep them in place.

Sources: http://inventors.about.com

Which of these accidental inventions do you think is the most interesting? the most useful?
Do you know of any other things that were invented accidentally?

2 PERSPECTIVES *It happened to me!*

A 🔊 Listen to what happened to these people. Check (✓) the things that have happened to you.

☐ "I was watching a really good movie, but I fell asleep before the end."

☐ "I was traveling in another country when I met an old school friend."

☐ "While I was shopping one day, a celebrity walked into the store."

☐ "I was talking to my friend when my cell phone died."

☐ "I was getting off a bus when I slipped and fell on the sidewalk."

☐ "I was typing my book report on my computer when it crashed."

☐ "While I was walking down the street, I found some money."

B Choose one statement that you checked. What happened next?

"I recharged my cell phone and called my friend back."

3 GRAMMAR FOCUS

> ### Past continuous vs. simple past ▶
>
> *Use the past continuous for an action in progress in the past.*
> *Use the simple past for an action that interrupts it.*
>
> I **was watching** a good movie, but I **fell** asleep before the end.
> I **was talking** to my friend when my cell phone **died**.
> While I **was shopping** one day, a celebrity **walked** into the store.

A Complete these sentences. Then compare with a partner.

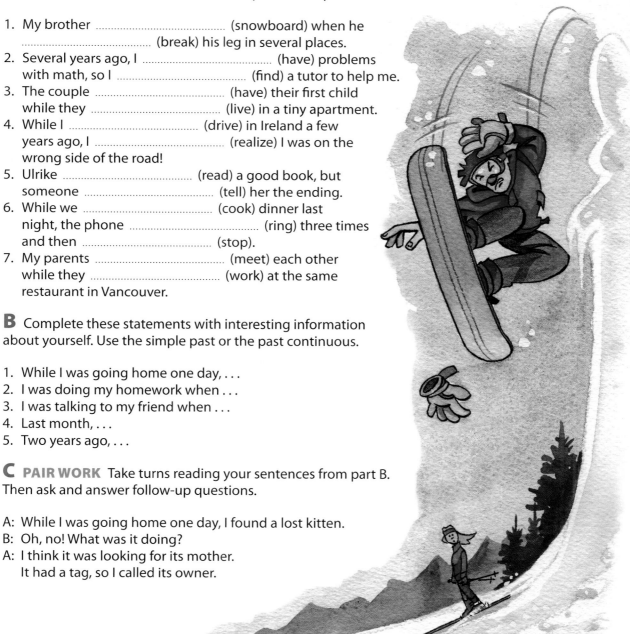

1. My brother .... (snowboard) when he
   .... (break) his leg in several places.
2. Several years ago, I .... (have) problems
   with math, so I .... (find) a tutor to help me.
3. The couple .... (have) their first child
   while they .... (live) in a tiny apartment.
4. While I .... (drive) in Ireland a few
   years ago, I .... (realize) I was on the
   wrong side of the road!
5. Ulrike .... (read) a good book, but
   someone .... (tell) her the ending.
6. While we .... (cook) dinner last
   night, the phone .... (ring) three times
   and then .... (stop).
7. My parents .... (meet) each other
   while they .... (work) at the same
   restaurant in Vancouver.

B Complete these statements with interesting information
about yourself. Use the simple past or the past continuous.

1. While I was going home one day, . . .
2. I was doing my homework when . . .
3. I was talking to my friend when . . .
4. Last month, . . .
5. Two years ago, . . .

C **PAIR WORK** Take turns reading your sentences from part B.
Then ask and answer follow-up questions.

A: While I was going home one day, I found a lost kitten.
B: Oh, no! What was it doing?
A: I think it was looking for its mother.
   It had a tag, so I called its owner.

4 LISTENING Lucky breaks

A ▶ Listen to these stories about lucky breaks. What were the people doing before they got their lucky breaks? What were their lucky breaks?

	What they were doing	Lucky break
1. Yang Zhifa	....	....
2. Gwyneth Paltrow	....	....

Terracotta warriors

B ▶ Listen again. How did the events change their lives?

5 WORD POWER Storytelling

A Some adverbs are often used in storytelling to emphasize that something interesting is about to happen. Which of these adverbs are positive (**P**)? Which are negative (**N**)? Which could be either (**E**)?

coincidentally	....	strangely	....
fortunately	....	suddenly	....
luckily	....	surprisingly	....
miraculously	....	unexpectedly	....
sadly	....	unfortunately	....

B **PAIR WORK** Complete these statements with adverbs from part A to make up creative sentences.

I was walking down the street when, . . .
It started out as a normal day, but, . . .
We were on our way to the party when, . . .

A: I was walking down the street when, unexpectedly, I saw a celebrity!
B: Or, I was walking down the street when, suddenly, I looked down and found $20!

6 WRITING A recent event

A Write a short story about something that happened to you recently. Try to include some of the adverbs from Exercise 5.

> I was visiting the coast last year when, unexpectedly, I got a chance to go kayaking. Fortunately, it was a perfect day, and I was having a great time. The water was calm, and I was beginning to feel a little tired when, suddenly, . . .

B **GROUP WORK** Take turns reading your stories. Answer any questions from the group.

7 CONVERSATION *What have you been doing?*

A ▶ Listen and practice.

Pete: Hey, Gina! I haven't seen you in ages. What have you been doing lately?

Gina: Nothing exciting. I've been working two jobs for the last six months.

Pete: How come?

Gina: I'm saving up money for a trip to Morocco.

Pete: Well, that's exciting.

Gina: Yeah, it is. What about you?

Pete: Well, I've only been *spending* money. I'm pursuing a full-time modeling career.

Gina: Really? How long have you been modeling?

Pete: Since I graduated. But I haven't been getting any work lately. I need a job soon. I'm almost out of money!

B ▶ Listen to two other people at the party. What has happened since they last saw each other?

8 GRAMMAR FOCUS

> ### Present perfect continuous ▶
>
> *Use the present perfect continuous for actions that start in the past and continue into the present.*
>
> What **have** you **been doing** lately?   I**'ve been working** two jobs for the last six months.
> How long **have** you **been modeling**?   I**'ve been modeling** since I graduated.
> **Have** you **been saving** money?   No, I **haven't been saving** money. I**'ve been spending** it!

A Complete the conversations with the present perfect continuous.

1. A: What .... you .... (do) lately?
   B: Well, I .... (spend) my free time at the beach.

2. A: .... you .... (work) part-time this year?
   B: Yes, I have. I .... (make) sandwiches at the Lunch Time Café for the past few months.

3. A: How .... you .... (feel) recently?
   B: Great! I .... (get) a lot of sleep. And I .... (not drink) as much coffee since I stopped working at the coffee shop.

4. A: .... you .... (get) enough exercise lately?
   B: No, I haven't. I .... (study) a lot for a big exam.

B **PAIR WORK** Read the conversations in part A together. Then read them again and answer the questions with your own information.

A: What have you been doing lately?
B: I've been listening to a lot of classical music. It helps me study.

What happened? ■ **81**

9 PRONUNCIATION *Contrastive stress in responses*

A ▶ Listen and practice. Notice how the stress changes to emphasize a contrast.

A: Has your brother been studying German?

B: No, I've been studying German.

A: Have you been teaching French?

B: No, I've been studying French.

B ▶ Mark the stress changes in these conversations. Listen and check. Then practice the conversations.

A: Have you been studying for ten years?

B: No, I've been studying for two years.

A: Have you been studying at school?

B: No, I've been studying at home.

10 SPEAKING *Tell me about it.*

GROUP WORK Add three questions to this list. Then take turns asking and answering the questions. Remember to ask for further information.

Have you been . . . lately?

taking any lessons
working out
learning a new hobby
working long hours
reading any good books
playing any cool video games
traveling
staying up late

....

....

....

useful expressions
Really?
I didn't know that!
Oh, I see.
I had no idea.
Wow! Tell me more.

A: Have you been taking any lessons lately?
B: Yes, I have. I've been taking driving lessons.
C: Really? How's that going?
B: Great! I think I'm becoming an excellent driver.

11 INTERCHANGE 12 *Life is like a game!*

Play a board game. Go to Interchange 12 on page 126.

From the Streets to the Screen

> Skim the article. What makes Staff Benda Bilili different from other groups of musicians?

Staff Benda Bilili is a group of musicians from Kinshasa, Democratic Republic of Congo (DRC). They live on the streets of the city. The four original group members are all disabled and move around on homemade tricycles. The group was founded by guitar players Papa Ricky Likabu and Coco Ngambali. Other musicians refused to play with them because they couldn't dance. Later, a street kid, Roger Landu, joined them. He made his own musical instrument from a fish can, a piece of wood, and one guitar string – nothing more.

The group's music is classic Congolese rumba mixed with reggae and rhythm 'n' blues. Their lyrics contain a message to street people and disabled people: Be very strong. Papa Ricky believes that the only real handicaps are in the mind, not the body. He says the group's main musical influences come from the street: "We sleep there, eat there, rehearse there." They also play there. Every evening, the group performs in front of an audience near Kinshasa Zoo.

In 2004, two French filmmakers were working in the DRC when, by chance, they heard Staff Benda Bilili's music. They loved it so much that they spent the next five years making a documentary film about the group. In 2009, Staff Benda Bilili's first CD was released. It's called *Très Très Fort*, which means "very very strong." The group won the WOMEX (World Music Expo) Artist Award. Then, in 2010, the documentary *Benda Bilili!* was screened at the Cannes Film Festival, and the group played on the opening night.

Staff Benda Bilili wants to use its worldwide success to raise awareness about the problems of street people in Kinshasa and around the world.

A Read the article. Find the words in *italics* below in the article. Then match each word with its meaning.

....	1. *disabled*	a.	unexpectedly
....	2. *lyrics*	b.	make people think
....	3. *handicaps*	c.	things that make it hard to do what you want
....	4. *rehearse*	d.	words of a song
....	5. *by chance*	e.	unable to walk or move easily
....	6. *raise awareness*	f.	practice before performing in front of an audience

B Answer these questions. Then compare with a partner.

1. Where do the members of Staff Benda Bilili live? ....
2. Why do they use tricycles? ....
3. What kind of music do they play? ....
4. How did they become famous? ....
5. What message do they want to tell the world? ....

C **PAIR WORK** Discuss people you know who had a lot of problems and then became very successful.

Units 11–12 Progress check

SELF-ASSESSMENT

How well can you do these things? Check (✓) the boxes.

I can	Very well	OK	A little
Give information about books, movies, songs, etc. (Ex. 1)	☐	☐	☐
Understand information about countries (Ex. 2)	☐	☐	☐
Describe a situation (Ex. 3)	☐	☐	☐
Ask and answer questions about past events (Ex. 4, 5)	☐	☐	☐
Ask and answer questions about recent activities (Ex. 5)	☐	☐	☐

1 SPEAKING *Right or wrong?*

A List six books, movies, songs, albums, or other popular works.
Then write one *who* question for each of the six items.

> The *X-Men* movies
> Who played Wolverine in the *X-Men* movies?

B **PAIR WORK** Take turns asking your questions.
Use the passive with *by* to answer.

A: Who played Wolverine in the *X-Men* movies?
B: I think Wolverine was played by Hugh Jackman.

2 LISTENING *Facts about Spain*

A ▶ Listen to people on a game show answer questions about Spain.
What are the answers? Complete the chart.

1. Currency	....	4. A popular sport	....
2. Country to the west	....	5. Two main crops	....
3. Capital	....	6. Two industries	....

B ▶ Listen again. Keep score. How much money does each contestant have?

GAME *Sentence-making competition*

GROUP WORK Use the passive to write details about these situations. Then compare with the class. Which group wrote the most sentences?

| Your roommate cleaned the apartment. | There was a big storm yesterday. | Someone broke into your house last night. |

| The dishes were done. | The airport was closed. | The window was broken. |

 ROLE PLAY *Alibis*

A famous painting has been stolen from a local museum. It disappeared last Sunday afternoon between 12 P.M. and 4 P.M.

Student A: Student B suspects you stole the painting. Make up an alibi. Take notes on what you were doing that day. Then answer Student B's questions.

Student B: You are a police detective. You think Student A stole the painting. Add two questions to the notebook. Then ask Student A the questions.

Change roles and try the role play again.

Where were you last Sunday?

Did you eat lunch? Who was with you?

What were you wearing that day?

What were you doing between noon and 4 p.m.?

Was anyone with you?

_____

_____

 DISCUSSION *Really? How interesting.*

A **GROUP WORK** What interesting things can you find out about your classmates? Ask these questions and others of your own.

Have you been doing anything exciting recently?
Are you studying anything right now? How long have you been studying it?
Have you met anyone interesting lately?
Who is your best friend? How did you meet?
Where were you living ten years ago? Did you like it there? What do you remember about it?

useful expressions
Really?
I didn't know that!
Oh, I see.
I had no idea.
Wow! Tell me more.

B **CLASS ACTIVITY** Tell the class the most interesting thing you learned.

WHAT'S NEXT?

Look at your Self-assessment again. Do you need to review anything?

13 Good book, terrible movie!

1 SNAPSHOT

Movie Trivia

- **Batman** (1989) The role of Batman was played by Michael Keaton. In later movies, it was played by Val Kilmer, George Clooney, and Christian Bale.
- **Titanic** (1997) The movie cost $200 million to make. The *Titanic* itself cost about $135 million to build.
- **Pirates of the Caribbean: The Curse of the Black Pearl** (2003) Keira Knightley nearly missed the audition because of a traffic jam.
- **Harry Potter and the Order of the Phoenix** (2007) This is the longest book and the shortest movie in the series.
- **Paranormal Activity** (2007) This movie only cost $15,000 to make, but it made $9.1 million in its first week.
- **Avatar** (2009) The special effects were so expensive that director James Cameron had to wait ten years to make the movie.
- **The Three Stooges** (2012) Jim Carrey, Sean Penn, and Benicio del Toro were originally cast in the film, but all three dropped out.

Source: www.imdb.com

Which of the movie trivia do you find most interesting?
Do you know any other movie trivia?
Which of the movies have you seen? Did you enjoy them?

2 CONVERSATION *What's playing?*

A ▶ Listen and practice.

Roger: Do you want to see a movie tonight?
Carol: Hmm. Maybe. What's playing?
Roger: How about the new *Star Trek* film? I hear it's really exciting.
Carol: Actually, the last one was boring.
Roger: What about the movie based on Stephen King's new novel?
Carol: I don't know. His books are usually fascinating, but I don't like horror movies.
Roger: Well, what do you want to see?
Carol: I'm interested in the new Sandra Bullock movie. It looks good.
Roger: That's fine with me. She's a wonderful actress.

B ▶ Listen to the rest of the conversation. What happens next? What do they decide to do?

Sandra Bullock

3 GRAMMAR FOCUS

> ## Participles as adjectives ▶
>
> **Present participles**
> Stephen King's books are **fascinating**.
> The last *Star Trek* film was **boring**.
> The new Sandra Bullock movie
>   sounds **interesting**.
>
> **Past participles**
> I'm **fascinated** by Stephen King's books.
> I was **bored** by the last *Star Trek* film.
> I'm **interested** in the new Sandra
>   Bullock movie.

A Complete these sentences. Then compare with a partner.

1. Matt Damon is an .... actor. (amaze)
2. I find animated films .... (amuse)
3. I'm not .... in science fiction movies. (interest)
4. I'm .... by watching television. (bore)
5. The final *Twilight* book was .... (excite)
6. I'm .... by J.R.R. Tolkien's novels. (fascinate)
7. It's .... that horror movies are so popular. (surprise)

Matt Damon

B **PAIR WORK** Complete the description below with the correct form of these words.

amaze   annoy   confuse   disgust   embarrass   shock

I had a terrible time at the movies last weekend. First, my ticket cost $15. I was really
.... by the price. By mistake, I gave the cashier two $5 bills instead of
a ten and a five. I was a little .... Then there was trash all over the theater.
The mess was .... The people behind me were talking during the movie,
which was .... The story was hard to follow. I always find thrillers
so .... I liked the special effects, though. They were .... !

4 WORD POWER Opinions

A **PAIR WORK** Complete the chart with synonyms from the list.

absurd	dumb	marvelous	silly
bizarre	fabulous	odd	terrible
disgusting	fantastic	outstanding	unusual
dreadful	horrible	ridiculous	weird

Awful	Wonderful	Stupid	Strange
....	....	....	....
....	....	....	....
....	....	....	....
....	....	....	....

B **GROUP WORK** Share your opinions about a movie, an actor,
an actress, a TV show, and a book. Use words from part A.

5 LISTENING How did you like it?

A Listen to people talk about books, movies, and TV programs. Which ones do you think they would recommend?

B Listen again. Check (✓) the adjective that best describes what the people say about each one.

1. ☐ fascinating 2. ☐ wonderful 3. ☐ boring 4. ☐ ridiculous
   ☐ silly   ☐ odd   ☐ terrific   ☐ interesting
   ☐ strange   ☐ boring   ☐ dreadful   ☐ exciting

6 PRONUNCIATION Emphatic stress

A Listen and practice. Notice how stress and a higher pitch are used to express strong opinions.

That was terrible!   He was amazing!   That's fascinating!

B PAIR WORK Write four statements using these words. Then take turns reading them. Pay attention to emphatic stress.

dreadful   fantastic   horrible   ridiculous

7 DISCUSSION Let's go to the movies!

A PAIR WORK Take turns asking and answering these questions and others of your own.

What kinds of movies are you interested in? Why?
What kinds of movies do you find boring?
Who are your favorite actors and actresses? Why?
Are there actors or actresses you don't like?
What's the worst movie you've ever seen?
What are your three favorite movies in
   English? Why?
Are there any outstanding movies playing now?

A: What kinds of movies are you interested in?
B: I love action movies.
A: Really? Why is that?
B: They're exciting! What about you?
A: I think action movies are kind of silly. I prefer . . .

B GROUP WORK Compare your information. Whose taste in movies is most like yours?

NOW SHOWING on DVD
COMEDIES
THRILLERS
DRAMA
MYSTERIES
ACTION / ADVENTURE
SCIENCE FICTION
Romance
CLASSICS
DOCUMENTARIES
HORROR
ANIMATION

8 PERSPECTIVES *It's about...*

A ▶ Listen to people talk about some of their Hollywood favorites. Can you guess the actress, actor, or movie each person is describing?

1. This action movie came out in 2010 and stars Leonardo DiCaprio as a thief who is able to steal information from people's minds. It's kind of confusing, but the special effects are amazing.

2. He's an actor who often plays unusual characters. He's fantastic as the Mad Hatter in *Alice in Wonderland* and Captain Jack Sparrow in the *Pirates of the Caribbean* movies.

3. It's a science fiction movie that was directed by James Cameron. It's a beautiful film that takes place on the moon Pandora in the year 2154. It's a story about the clash of cultures and civilizations.

4. She's an actress who is excellent in both dramas and comedies. I loved her in *Mamma Mia!* and *The Iron Lady*. I haven't seen a lot of her earlier movies, though.

B Do you like the people and movies described in part A? What else do you know about them?

9 GRAMMAR FOCUS

Relative pronouns for people and things ▶

Use who or that for people.

He's an actor. He often plays unusual characters.

He's an actor **who/that** often plays unusual characters.

Use which or that for things.

It's a movie. It stars Leonardo DiCaprio.

It's a movie **which/that** stars Leonardo DiCaprio.

A Combine the sentences using relative pronouns. Then compare with a partner.

1. *Super Mario Galaxy 2* is a video game. It's fun for all ages.
2. Jodie Foster is an actress. She began her career at age three.
3. Ben Affleck is an actor. He's also a director.
4. *The Lorax* is a film. It was adapted from a children's book.
5. Jaden Smith is an actor. He's the son of Will Smith.
6. Dan Brown writes books. They're hard to put down.
7. *Wicked* is a Broadway musical. It's been very successful.
8. Beyoncé is a singer. She's acted in several films.

B **PAIR WORK** Complete these sentences. Then compare your information around the class.

1. Cameron Diaz is an actress . . .
2. *Toy Story 3* is a movie . . .
3. Justin Bieber is a singer . . .
4. *The Simpsons* is a TV show . . .

10 INTERCHANGE 13 *Famous faces*

What do you know about movies and TV shows? Go to Interchange 13 on page 127.

11 SPEAKING A new TV show

A **PAIR WORK** A TV studio is looking for ideas for a new
TV show. Brainstorm possible ideas and agree on an idea.
Make brief notes.

What kind of TV show is it?
What's it about?
Who are the main characters?
Who will it appeal to?

B **CLASS ACTIVITY** Tell the class about your TV show.

"Our TV show is a detective story. It's about two
secret agents who are chasing an alien from
another planet. There are two main characters. . . ."

12 LISTENING A night at the movies

A ▶ Listen to two critics talk about a new movie. What do they like
or not like about it? Rate each item in the chart from 1 to 3.

	Acting	Story	Music	Special effects
Pauline	....	....	....	....
Colin	....	....	....	....

Ratings
1 = didn't like it
2 = OK
3 = liked it very much

B ▶ Look at the chart in part A. Guess how many stars each
critic gave the movie. Then listen to the critics give their ratings.

★ poor   ★★ fair   ★★★ good   ★★★★ excellent

13 WRITING A movie review

A **PAIR WORK** Choose a movie you both
have seen and discuss it. Then write a
review of it.

What was the movie about?
What did you like about it?
What didn't you like about it?
How was the acting?
How would you rate it?

B **CLASS ACTIVITY** Read your review to
the class. Who else has seen the movie?
Do they agree with your review?

Rate ★★★★★   @ Email   Search [____] Go

👥 WATCH TRAILER   f t +1 412

We recently saw the
2011 film *Water for
Elephants* on DVD. It's
about a man who joins
a traveling circus as a
veterinarian in the
1930s. It stars Robert
Pattinson and Reese
Witherspoon. It was
adapted from a book
by the same name. I like this movie because the story
is both funny and sad. I didn't like... **More**

SPECIAL EFFECTS

Scan the article. What is the most important change in special effects?

1 Nowadays, almost anything can happen in the movies. Dinosaurs rule the world, people fly, and aliens attack spacecraft. But how is it all possible?

2 Special effects started long before the movies. For centuries, magicians performed in the streets, usually in markets and fairs. They did card tricks and things like making rabbits "disappear." In the early nineteenth century, before the invention of electricity, actors in theaters were highlighted by limelights. Sometime later, a lighting technique called "Pepper's ghost" was used to make ghosts "appear" on stage. Audiences were thrilled.

3 Motion pictures began in the 1890s, but there was no sound. They were "silent movies." "Talkies" were first shown in the 1920s. Later, color films gradually replaced black-and-white ones.

4 From the 1950s to the 1980s, special effects became more and more fantastic. Experts in robotics, computers, engineering, and other fields were employed by filmmakers. However, the biggest development in special effects came with computer-generated imagery (CGI) in the 1990s. *Jurassic Park* (1993) had full shots of dinosaurs using CGI. *Titanic* (1997) used CGI for shots on board the ship and very small models to show underwater shots of the ship.

5 More recently, *Avatar* (2009) used 60 percent CGI and 40 percent live action. It was the first film to be shot entirely with a 3-D camera. It shows totally believable scenes of humans and aliens on the moon Pandora.

6 Special effects in movies are both a science and an art. Computer technology and human imagination come together to bring stories to life. They make science fiction and action movies much more exciting to watch, and audiences love them.

A Read the article. Then number these sentences from 1 (first event) to 9 (last event).

.... a. Silent movies were shown.
.... b. CGI was developed.
.... c. Limelights were used in theaters.
.... d. CGI was used to show dinosaurs.
.... e. Talkies began to replace silent movies.
.... f. Street magicians performed tricks.
.... g. Color movies were shown.
.... h. Small models and CGI were used in *Titanic*.
.... i. The first full movie was made with a 3-D camera.

B Where do these sentences belong? Write the number of the paragraph where each sentence should go.

.... a. It used the movie format IMAX 3-D.
.... b. Movies also show amazing things like meteors hitting the Earth.
.... c. This meant audiences could see the stage more clearly.
.... d. Models were used for shots of parts of dinosaurs.
.... e. Even if special effects are often very expensive, they are good for business.
.... f. One of the first films with sound was *The Jazz Singer*.

C **PAIR WORK** What movie do you think has the best special effects? Why do you like them?

So that's what it means!

1 SNAPSHOT

Popular Emoticons

:-)	I'm happy.			#-)	I'm sleepy.
:-(	I'm sad.	(:+(	That was scary!	:-9	That was delicious!
}:[	I'm angry.	:-X	I can't talk about it.	:-~(	I have a terrible cold.
;-)	Just kidding!	:-/	Really? That can't be right!	:-&	I don't know what to say!
:-D	That's funny!	:-O	I'm surprised!	:-|	I'm so bored.

Source: www.computeruser.com

Do people in your country use emoticons? Do you?
What other emoticons can you use to communicate these ideas?
What other emoticons do you know?

2 WORD POWER *Feelings and gestures*

A What is this man doing in each picture? Match each description with a picture. Then compare with a partner.

1. He's biting his nails. ....
2. He's rolling his eyes. ....
3. He's scratching his head. ....
4. He's tapping his foot. ....
5. He's twirling his hair. ....
6. He's wrinkling his nose. ....

B GROUP WORK Use the pictures in part A and these adjectives to describe how the man is feeling.

annoyed	confused	embarrassed	frustrated	irritated
bored	disgusted	exhausted	impatient	nervous

"In the first picture, he's twirling his hair. He looks nervous."

3 CONVERSATION *Have you met Raj?*

A ▶ Listen and practice.

Ron: Have you met Raj, the student from India?
Emily: No, I haven't.
Ron: Well, he seems really nice, but there's one thing I noticed. He moves his head from side to side when you talk to him. You know, like this.
Emily: Maybe it means he doesn't understand you.
Ron: No, I don't think so.
Emily: Or it could mean he doesn't agree with you.
Peter: Actually, people from India sometimes move their heads from side to side when they agree with you.
Ron: Oh, so that's what it means!

B ▶ Now listen to Raj talk to his friend. What does he find unusual about the way people in North America communicate?

4 GRAMMAR FOCUS

> ### Modals and adverbs ▶
>
> **Modals**
> It **might/may** mean he doesn't understand you.
>
> It **could** mean he doesn't agree with you.
>
> That **must** mean he agrees with you.
>
> **Adverbs**
> **Maybe/Perhaps** it means he doesn't understand you.
>
> It **possibly/probably** means he doesn't agree with you.
>
> That **definitely** means he agrees with you.

PAIR WORK What do these gestures mean? Take turns making statements about each gesture using the meanings in the box.

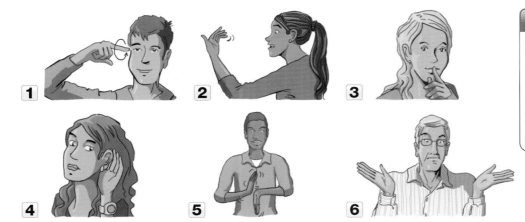

1   **2**   **3**

4   **5**   **6**

possible meanings

I don't know.
Be quiet.
I'm finished.
That sounds crazy!
I can't hear you.
Come here.

A: What do you think the first gesture means?
B: It probably means . . . , or it might mean . . .

5 SPEAKING What does it mean?

A PAIR WORK Imagine you are in a foreign country and you don't speak the language. Think of gestures to communicate these meanings.

Go away.	I don't understand.
Help!	It's delicious.
Please repeat.	How much does this cost?
I'm lost.	Someone stole my wallet.
I'm hungry.	Where's the bathroom?

B CLASS ACTIVITY What else could your gestures mean? For each gesture you acted out in part A, think of one more possible meaning.

A: That probably means "go away," but it might also mean you don't like something.
B: It could also mean . . .

6 PRONUNCIATION Pitch

A Listen and practice. Notice how pitch is used to express certainty or doubt.

	Certain	**Uncertain**
A: Do you think her gesture means "go away"?	B: Definitely.	B: Probably.
A: Do you understand what her gesture means?	B: Absolutely.	B: Maybe.

B PAIR WORK Take turns asking yes/no questions. Respond by using *absolutely, definitely, maybe, probably,* and your own information. Pay attention to pitch.

7 INTERCHANGE 14 What's going on?

Interpret people's body language. Go to Interchange 14 on page 128.

8 PERSPECTIVES *Signs*

A ▶ What do you think these international signs mean? Listen and match each sign with the correct meaning.

1. .... 2. .... 3. .... 4. .... 5. .... 6. .... 7. .... 8. ....

a. You can camp here.
b. You aren't allowed to take photos here.
c. You have to fasten your seat belts.
d. You can recycle this item.

e. You have to wear a hard hat to enter this area.
f. You can't drink the water here. It's not safe.
g. You have to keep your dog on a leash here.
h. You've got to take off your shoes here.

B PAIR WORK Where might you see the signs in part A? Give two suggestions for each one.

"You might see this one at a national park or . . ."

9 GRAMMAR FOCUS

Permission, obligation, and prohibition ▶

Permission	Obligation	Prohibition
You **can** camp here.	You **have to** camp here.	You **can't** camp here.
You'**re allowed to** take off your shoes.	You'**ve got to** take off your shoes.	You **aren't allowed to** take off your shoes.

A Match these school rules with the correct sign. Then compare with a partner.

1. Lock your bikes in the bike rack. ....
2. No eating or drinking in the classroom. ....
3. No playing ball in the hallway. ....
4. Keep the classroom door closed. ....
5. No listening to music. ....
6. Throw trash in the wastebasket. ....
7. No cell phones. ....
8. Turn out the lights when leaving. ....

a

b

c

d

e

f

g

h

B PAIR WORK Use the language in the grammar box to take turns talking about each sign.

A: This first sign means you aren't allowed to eat or drink in the classroom.
B: Yes, I think you're right. And the second one means you have to . . .

10 DISCUSSION Rules and regulations

A PAIR WORK How many rules can you think of for each of these places?

on an airplane   in an art museum   on a bus or subway
in a library   in a movie theater   at work

"On an airplane, you have to wear your seat belt when
the plane is taking off and landing."

B GROUP WORK Share your ideas. Why do you think these
rules exist? Have you ever broken any of them? What happened?

11 LISTENING Sign language

A ▶ Listen to three conversations about driving. Check (✓) True or False
for each statement.

	True	False
1. The man hasn't had a parking ticket lately.	☐	☐
Parking isn't allowed there during working hours.	☐	☐
The fine for parking is $16.	☐	☐
2. The woman is driving faster than the speed limit.	☐	☐
There are other cars in her lane.	☐	☐
The lane is reserved for buses and taxis.	☐	☐
3. The other drivers are flashing their lights.	☐	☐
He's driving with his lights on.	☐	☐
The other drivers are giving him a warning.	☐	☐

B ▶ Listen again. Which of the drivers did something wrong?

12 WRITING A list of rules

A GROUP WORK Discuss the rules that currently exist at your school.
How many can you think of? Are they all good rules?

B GROUP WORK Think of four new rules that you feel would be a good idea.
Work together to write brief explanations of why each is necessary.

> 1. You aren't allowed to chew gum in class because it may bother other students.
> 2. You can be late, but you have to come in quietly so you don't disturb the lesson.
> 3. You have to pay a small fine if your cell phone rings in class because . . .

C CLASS ACTIVITY Share your lists. Vote on the best new rules.

Pearls of Wisdom

Look at these proverbs and the pictures below. Then match each proverb with a picture.

ⓐ *A bird in the hand is worth two in the bush.*

ⓑ *One person's meat is another one's poison.*

ⓒ *Don't count your chickens before they hatch.*

ⓓ *Money doesn't grow on trees.*

1 **Why do people use proverbs?** Many people love proverbs for their wisdom. Others enjoy the images in proverbs. But proverbs are most impressive because they express a lot of information in just a few words. A good proverb quickly sums up ideas that are sometimes hard to express. And the person listening immediately understands the message.

2 **Where do proverbs come from?** Proverbs come from two main places – ordinary people and famous people. These two sources are not always distinct. Common and popular wisdom has often been used by famous people.

And something said or written down by a well-known person has often been borrowed by the common man. For example, "Bad news travels fast" probably comes from the experience of housewives. However, "All's well that ends well" was written by William Shakespeare.

3 **What do proverbs tell us?** Proverbs are used everywhere in the world. If you can understand a culture's proverbs, you can better understand the culture itself. There are many different ways that we use proverbs in daily life. Here are some examples of what proverbs can do:

Give advice
Meaning: Something you have is better than something you might get.

Give a warning
Meaning: Don't plan on a successful outcome until it actually happens.

Teach a lesson
Meaning: It's not easy to get money.

Express a common truth
Meaning: What one person loves, another person may hate.

A Read the article. Then find these sentences in the article. Decide whether each sentence is the main idea or a supporting idea in that paragraph. Check (✓) the correct boxes.

	Main idea	Supporting idea
1. Many people love proverbs for their wisdom. (par. 1)	☐	☐
2. But proverbs are most . . . just a few words. (par. 1)	☐	☐
3. Proverbs come from . . . and famous people. (par. 2)	☐	☐
4. If you can understand . . . the culture itself. (par. 3)	☐	☐
5. There are many . . . proverbs in daily life. (par. 3)	☐	☐

B **CLASS ACTIVITY** Think of an interesting proverb from your country. What does it mean? Tell it to the class in English.

Units 13–14 Progress check

SELF-ASSESSMENT

How well can you do these things? Check (✓) the boxes.

I can	Very well	OK	A little
Ask about and express opinions and emotions (Ex. 1, 4, 5)	☐	☐	☐
Describe people and things (Ex. 2)	☐	☐	☐
Understand speculations and recognize emotions (Ex. 3, 4)	☐	☐	☐
Speculate about things when I'm not sure (Ex. 3, 4)	☐	☐	☐
Describe rules and laws: permission, obligation, and prohibition (Ex. 5)	☐	☐	☐

 SURVEY *Entertainment opinions*

A Complete the first column of the survey with your opinions.

	Me	My classmate
A confusing movie	....	....
A boring TV show	....	....
A shocking news story	....	....
A fascinating book	....	....
An interesting celebrity	....	....
A singer you are amazed by	....	....
A song you are annoyed by	....	....

B **CLASS ACTIVITY** Go around the class and find someone who has the same opinions. Write a classmate's name only once.

"I thought *Inception* was a confusing movie. What about you?"

2 ROLE PLAY *Movie recommendations*

Student A: Invite Student B to a movie. Suggest two films.
Then answer your partner's questions.
Start like this: *Do you want to see a movie?*

Student B: Student A invites you to a movie. Find out more about the movie. Then accept or refuse the invitation.

Change roles and try the role play again.

3 LISTENING *That's how I feel!*

A ▶ Listen to some people talking. Write what each person is talking about.

1. .... 2. .... 3. .... 4. ....

B ▶ Listen again. What does each person mean? Check (✓) the best answer.

1. ☐ He is confused.
   ☐ He is nervous.

2. ☐ She enjoyed it.
   ☐ She hated it.

3. ☐ He didn't understand it.
   ☐ He thought it was interesting.

4. ☐ She is frustrated.
   ☐ She is bored.

4 GAME *Charades*

A Think of two emotions or ideas you can communicate with gestures. Write them on separate cards.

> I'm tired of waiting.

B **GROUP WORK** Shuffle your cards together. Then take turns picking cards and acting out the meanings with gestures. The student who guesses correctly goes next.

A: That probably means you're bored.
B: No.
C: It could mean you're impatient.
B: You're getting closer. . . .

5 DISCUSSION *What's the law?*

GROUP WORK Read these laws from the United States. What do you think about them? Are they the same or different in your country?

- You're allowed to vote when you turn 18.
- In some states, you can get married when you're 16.
- You have to wear a seat belt in the front seat of a car.
- Young men don't have to serve in the military.
- You aren't allowed to keep certain wild animals as pets.
- In some states, you can't drive faster than 65 miles per hour (about 100 kph).
- You have to have a passport to enter the country.

A: In the U.S., you're allowed to vote when you turn 18.
B: That's surprising! In my country, we *have* to vote when we're 18.
C: And in my country, we *can't* vote until we're 20.

WHAT'S NEXT?

Look at your Self-assessment again. Do you need to review anything?

15 What would you do?

1 SNAPSHOT

The Morning News

HOME　CURRENT ISSUE　ARCHIVES　WEB EXTRAS　RADIO　CONTACT US　SUBSCRIBE

Stories of Honesty

Businessman returns $750,000 to owner – and is thanked with a brief phone call

READ MORE ➕

Athlete admits to cheating – confesses that he "just wanted to win"

READ MORE ➕

Taxi driver returns computer – drives miles to give laptop back to passenger

READ MORE ➕

Golfer admits using illegal ball by mistake – but is still disqualified from game

READ MORE ➕

Student uses detective work to find owner of gold jewelry

READ MORE ➕

Fan returns soccer star's lucky T-shirt – player gives him $1,000 reward

READ MORE ➕

Sources: www.geardiary.com; http://sports.espn.go.com; *Los Angeles Times*

Do you know any other stories like these?
Have you ever found anything valuable? What did you do?
Do you think that people who return lost things should get a reward?

2 CONVERSATION *If I found $750,000, . . .*

A ▶ Listen and practice.

Phil: Look at this. Some guy found $750,000! He returned it, and the owner simply thanked him with a phone call.

Pat: You're kidding! If I found $750,000, I wouldn't return it so fast.

Phil: Why? What would you do?

Pat: Well, I'd go out and start spending it. I could buy lots of nice clothes and jewelry.

Phil: Someone might also find out about it. And then you could go to jail.

Pat: Hmm. You've got a point there.

B ▶ Listen to the rest of the conversation. What would Phil do if he found $750,000?

3 GRAMMAR FOCUS

Unreal conditional sentences with if clauses ⊙

Imaginary situation (simple past)	Possible consequence (would, could, or might + verb)
If I **found** $750,000,	I **would spend** it.
	I **wouldn't return** it so fast.
	I **could buy** lots of nice clothes and jewelry.
	I **might go** to the police.

What **would** you **do if** you **found** $750,000?

A Complete these conversations. Then compare with a partner.

1. A: If you .... (have) three months to travel, where .... you .... (go)?
   B: Oh, that's easy! I .... (fly) to Europe. I've always wanted to go there.

2. A: If your doctor .... (tell) you to get more exercise, which sport .... you .... (choose)?
   B: I'm not sure, but I .... (go) jogging two or three times a week.

3. A: What .... you .... (do) if your teacher .... (give) you an A by mistake?
   B: Of course I .... (say) something right away.

4. A: .... you .... (break) into your house if you .... (lock) yourself out?
   B: If I .... (not have) another key, I .... (ask) a neighbor for help.

5. A: If your friend .... (want) to marry someone you didn't trust, ... you .... (say) something?
   B: No, I .... (not say) anything. I .... (mind) my own business.

6. A: What .... you .... (do) if you .... (see) your favorite movie star on the street?
   B: I .... (not be) shy! I .... (ask) for a photo and an autograph.

B **PAIR WORK** Take turns asking the questions in part A. Answer with your own information.

4 LISTENING Tough predicaments

A ⊙ Listen to three people talk about predicaments. Number them from 1 to 3 in the order they are discussed.

Predicament	Suggestions
☐ Two people were fighting in the street.	....
☐ A friend lost all her money while traveling.	....
☐ A friend has a serious shopping problem.	....

B ⊙ Listen again. What suggestions do the people give for each predicament? Take notes. Which is the best suggestion?

5 INTERCHANGE 15 *Do the right thing!*

What would you do in some difficult situations? Go to Interchange 15 on page 130.

6 WORD POWER *Opposites*

A Find nine pairs of opposites in this list. Complete the chart.
Then compare with a partner.

✓ accept	borrow	dislike	find	lose	remember
admit	deny	divorce	forget	marry	save
agree	disagree	enjoy	lend	✓ refuse	spend

accept	≠	refuse		≠			≠	
	≠			≠			≠	
	≠			≠			≠	

B PAIR WORK Choose four pairs of opposites. Write sentences using each pair.

> I can never save money because I spend it all on clothes.

7 PERSPECTIVES *I felt terrible.*

A ◉ Listen to people talk about recent predicaments.
Then check (✓) the best suggestion for each one.

❝What a disaster! I spilled juice on my parents' new couch. They weren't home, so I just turned the cushions over. What should I have done?❞

☐ You should have told them about it.

☐ You should have cleaned it immediately.

☐ You should have offered to buy them a new couch.

❝I forgot my best friend's birthday. I felt terrible, so I sent him a text to apologize. What would you have done?❞

☐ I would have called him right away.

☐ I would have sent him a nice birthday present.

☐ I would have invited him out for a meal.

B PAIR WORK Compare with a partner. Do you agree with each other?

8 GRAMMAR FOCUS

Past modals ▶

Use would have or should have + past participle to give opinions or suggestions about actions in the past.

What **should** I **have done**?

What **would** you **have done**?

You **should have told** them about it.
You **shouldn't have hidden** it.
I **would have called** him.
I **wouldn't have sent** him a text.

A Complete these conversations. Then practice with a partner.

1. A: The cashier gave me too much change. What should I have .... (do)?
   B: You should have .... (say) something. You shouldn't have .... (take) the money.

2. A: I ignored an email from someone I don't like. What would you have .... (do)?
   B: I would have .... (reply) to the person. It just takes a minute!

3. A: I was watching a good movie when my phone rang. What should I have .... (do)?
   B: You should have .... (take) the call and .... (tell) the person you'd call back later.

4. A: We left all our trash at the campsite. What would you have .... (do)?
   B: I would have .... (take) it with me and .... (throw) it away later.

B Read the situations below. What would have been the best thing to do? Choose suggestions. Then compare with a partner.

Situations

1. The teacher borrowed my favorite book and spilled coffee all over it. ....
2. I saw a classmate cheating on an exam. So I wrote her an email about it. ....
3. A friend of mine always has messy hair. So I gave him a comb for his birthday. ....
4. I hit someone's car when I was leaving a parking lot. Luckily, no one saw me. ....
5. My aunt gave me a wool sweater. I can't wear wool, so I gave it back. ....

Suggestions

a. You should have spoken to him about it.
b. I would have spoken to the teacher about it.
c. I would have waited for the owner to return.
d. I wouldn't have said anything.
e. You should have warned her not to do it again.
f. You should have left a note for the owner.
g. I would have told her that I prefer something else.
h. You should have exchanged it for something else.

C GROUP WORK Make another suggestion for each situation in part B.

9 PRONUNCIATION Reduction of have

A ▶ Listen and practice. Notice how **have** is reduced in these sentences.

/əv/
What would you have done?

/əv/
I would have told the truth.

B PAIR WORK Practice the conversations in Exercise 8, part A, again. Use the reduced form of **have**.

10 LISTENING *I'm calling about . . .*

A ▶ Listen to people calling Dr. Hilda, a counselor on a radio talk show. Complete the chart.

	Problem	What the caller did
Caller 1	....	....
Caller 2	....	....
Caller 3	....	....

B ▶ Listen again. According to Dr. Hilda, what should each caller have done?

C GROUP WORK Do you agree with Dr. Hilda? What would you have done?

11 SPEAKING *I shouldn't have . . .*

A Look at the five situations below. Think about the past month and write down an example for each situation.

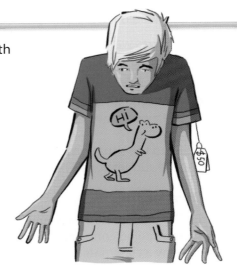

1. something you shouldn't have done
2. something you should have done
3. something you shouldn't have said
4. somewhere you shouldn't have gone
5. someone you should have emailed or called

B GROUP WORK Talk about each situation in part A.

"I spent $50 on a T-shirt. I shouldn't have bought it. I don't even like it now."

12 WRITING *A letter to an advice columnist*

Write a letter to an advice columnist about a real or imaginary problem.
Put your letters on the wall and choose one to write a reply to.

> Dear Dr. Hilda,
>
>   I let a friend borrow my laptop, and now it's not working very well. I took it to a repair shop, and they said it would be very expensive to fix. When I asked my friend to help me pay for the repair, she refused. Now she won't even speak to me! What did I do wrong? What should I have done? Thanks for your help!
>
> Kevin

The Advice Circle

Search [_____] [Go] 🐦Tweet 12 [f Like]

Login/Join

Skim the three posts on the message board. What problem does each writer have?

| Health | Parenting | Education | Lifestyle | **Relationships** |

Terry — Someone told me that my brother's girlfriend was dating another guy. I told my brother and he then decided to confront her with the story. They had an argument and, although she denied the rumor, they broke up. Now it turns out that the rumor wasn't true, and my brother isn't speaking to me. — Posts: 11

Pixie — You really learned a lesson, didn't you? You shouldn't have listened to gossip. Now you have to repair the damage. Apologize and hope that he will forgive and forget! — Posts: 14 — Hide Post

Lola — Don't blame yourself. You sincerely tried your best. But, frankly, I wouldn't have acted so quickly. I would have waited to see what happened. Try talking to him – and good luck! — Posts: 7 — Hide Post

Linda — My son is 23 and still lives at home. He finished college last year, but I really don't think he's trying to get a job. Meanwhile, I've been cooking his meals and doing his laundry. — Posts: 21

Too Bad — You're making it too easy for him to stay home. Be firm and tell him he has to find a job and get his own place. He's old enough to take care of himself. — Posts: 17 — Hide Post

Poodle — You're his mother, and family is family. It's hard to find a job if you have no experience. And don't you have to cook for yourself? Don't complain about your son. — Posts: 3 — Hide Post

Robin — I saw my friend's brother at the beach with some of his friends. It wasn't a holiday, so I think he was skipping school. Should I tell my friend? — Posts: 15

Zeb — I would suggest you keep your mouth shut. Let them work things out for themselves. If you say something, you could damage your friendship with both of them. — Posts: 27 — Hide Post

Speedy — What are you waiting for? You should tell your friend right now, and tell her mom, too! The only way to solve your dilemma is to be 100% honest. — Posts: 10 — Hide Post

A Read the message board. Match the name and the advice.

1. Pixie ....   a. Be honest.
2. Lola ....   b. Say nothing.
3. Too Bad ....   c. Be firm.
4. Poodle ....   d. Apologize.
5. Zeb ....   e. Talk to him.
6. Speedy ....   f. Don't complain.

B Find the words in *italics* below in the message board. Then match each one with its meaning.

.... 1. *confront*   a. make a fresh start
.... 2. *forgive and forget*   b. strong and determined
.... 3. *firm*   c. a difficult problem
.... 4. *dilemma*   d. discuss in a strong, direct way

C **PAIR WORK** Which advice do you agree or disagree with? What advice would you give?

16 What's your excuse?

1 SNAPSHOT

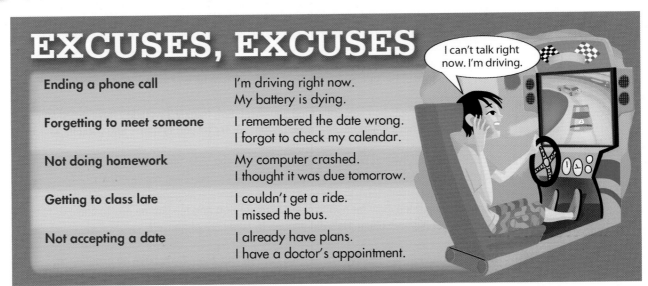

EXCUSES, EXCUSES

Ending a phone call	I'm driving right now. My battery is dying.
Forgetting to meet someone	I remembered the date wrong. I forgot to check my calendar.
Not doing homework	My computer crashed. I thought it was due tomorrow.
Getting to class late	I couldn't get a ride. I missed the bus.
Not accepting a date	I already have plans. I have a doctor's appointment.

I can't talk right now. I'm driving.

Source: Based on www.answers.yahoo.com

Have you ever heard any of these excuses? Have you ever used any of them?
Which are good excuses? Which are bad excuses?
What other excuses can you make for not accepting an invitation?

2 PERSPECTIVES *Who said it?*

A Who do you think made these requests? Listen and match.

1. He asked me to play my music more quietly.	**a.** my doctor
2. She told me not to stay out past midnight.	**b.** my coach
3. She said to drink at least six glasses of water a day.	**c.** my friend
4. He said not to be late for practice again.	**d.** my neighbor
5. She asked me to pick up the kids after school.	**e.** my mother
6. He told me to bring a dictionary tomorrow.	**f.** my wife
7. He asked me not to tell anyone about his new girlfriend.	**g.** my teacher

B **PAIR WORK** Can you think of another request each person might make?

A: A doctor might also tell a patient to get more exercise.
B: . . . or to avoid eating greasy foods.

106

3 GRAMMAR FOCUS

Reported speech: requests ⊙

Original request	Reported request
Bring a dictionary tomorrow.	He **said to bring** a dictionary tomorrow. He **told me to bring** a dictionary tomorrow.
Don't stay out past midnight.	She **said not to stay** out past midnight. She **told me not to stay** out past midnight.
Can you play your music more quietly?	He **asked me to play** my music more quietly.

A Amanda is having a surprise party for Albert. Look at what she told the guests. Write each request using *say, tell,* or *ask.* Then compare with a partner.

1. Meet at Albert's apartment at 7:30. _She told them to meet at Albert's apartment at 7:30._
2. Can you bring your favorite music? ....
3. Don't bring any food. ....
4. Can you bring a small gift for Albert? ....
5. Don't spend more than $10 on the gift. ....
6. Keep the party a secret. ....

B GROUP WORK Imagine you're planning a class party. Write four requests. Then take turns reading your requests and changing them into reported requests.

> Juan: Bring something good to eat to the party!
> Sonia: Juan told us to bring something good to eat.

> Noriko: Can you help me clean up after the party?
> Jin-sook: Noriko asked us to help her clean up.

4 SPEAKING *What a request!*

A Think of requests that people have made recently. Write two things people asked you to do and two things people asked you *not* to do.

Person	Request
my mom	get a haircut
....	....
....	....
....	....
....	....

B GROUP WORK Compare with others. Who has the most interesting or unusual requests?

5 WORD POWER *Verb and noun pairs*

A Find words or phrases in the list that are usually paired with each verb. Then compare with a partner.

✓ anger
✓ an apology
  a complaint
✓ a compliment
  a concern

✓ your congratulations
  a criticism
  an excuse
  an invitation
✓ a joke

a lie
a reason
your regrets
sympathy
the truth

express	anger	....	....
give	a compliment	....	....
make	an apology	....	....
offer	your congratulations	....	....
tell	a joke	....	....

B **PAIR WORK** In what situations do you do the things in part A?
Write five sentences about things you *never*, *sometimes*, or *always* do.
Then take turns reading your sentences and asking questions.

A: I never tell a lie.
B: Are you sure? What if someone invited you to a party, but you didn't want to go?

6 CONVERSATION *Are you doing anything on Saturday?*

A ▶ Listen and practice.

Albert: Hi, Daniel.
Daniel: Oh, hi, Albert. How are things?
Albert: Just fine, thanks. Uh, are you doing anything on Saturday night?
Daniel: Hmm. Saturday night? Let me think. Oh, yes. My cousin just called to say he was flying in that night. I told him I would pick him up.
Albert: Oh, that's too bad! It's my birthday. I'm having dinner with Amanda, and I thought I'd invite more people and make it a party.
Daniel: Gee, I'm really sorry, but I won't be able to make it.
Albert: I'm sorry, too. But that's OK.

B **PAIR WORK** Act out the conversation in part A. Make up your own excuse for not accepting Albert's invitation.

A ▶ Listen to Albert inviting friends to his party on Saturday. What excuses do people give for not coming? Match the person to the excuse.

1. Scott ....
2. Fumiko ....
3. Manuel ....
4. Regina ....

   a. She said that she wasn't feeling well.
   b. He said he was taking his mother to a dance club.
   c. She said she had houseguests for the weekend.
   d. He said that he would be out of town.
   e. She said she might go out with friends.
   f. He said he was going away with his family.

B ▶ Listen. What happens on the night of Albert's birthday?

8 **GRAMMAR FOCUS**

Reported speech: statements ▶

Direct statements	Reported statements	
I**'m not feeling** well.	She **said** (that)	she **wasn't feeling** well.
I **have** houseguests for the weekend.		she **had** houseguests for the weekend.
I **made** a tennis date with Kim.		she **had made** a tennis date with Kim.
I **have planned** an exciting trip.		she **had planned** an exciting trip.
We **can't come** tomorrow.	They **told me** (that)	they **couldn't come** tomorrow.
We **will be** out of town.		they **would be** out of town.
We **may go** out with friends.		they **might go** out with friends.

A Sandra is having a party at her house on Saturday. Look at these excuses. Change them into reported speech. Then compare with a partner.

1. Donna: "I have to babysit my nephew that night."
2. William and Brigitte: "We're going out of town for the weekend."
3. Mary: "I've been invited to a wedding on Saturday."
4. James: "I promised to help Dennis move."
5. Anita: "I can't come because I have the flu."
6. Mark: "I'll be studying for a test all weekend."
7. Eva and Randall: "We have to pick someone up at the airport that evening."
8. David: "I may have to work late on Saturday night."

> Donna said she had to babysit her nephew that night. OR
> Donna told her she had to babysit her nephew that night.

B **GROUP WORK** Imagine you don't want to go to Sandra's party. Take turns making excuses and changing them into reported speech.

A: I'm sorry I can't go. I have tickets to a concert that night.
B: Lucky guy! He said he had tickets to a concert that night.

9 PRONUNCIATION *Reduction of had and would*

A ▶ Listen and practice. Notice how **had** and **would** are reduced in the following sentences.

She said she**'d made** the bed. (She said she **had made** the bed.)
She said she**'d make** the bed. (She said she **would make** the bed.)

B ▶ Listen to four sentences. Check (✓) the reduced form that you hear.

1. ☐ had
   ☐ would
2. ☐ had
   ☐ would
3. ☐ had
   ☐ would
4. ☐ had
   ☐ would

10 WRITING *A report*

A Interview your classmates and take notes. Use your notes to write a report describing what people told you. Use reported speech.

	Name	Response
What did you do last weekend?	....	....
What new TV show have you seen recently?	....	....
Where are you going after class?	....	....
What are your plans this evening?	....	....
What will you do this weekend?	....	....

B **GROUP WORK** Read your report, but don't give names. Others guess the person.

"Someone told me that she'd watched three movies last weekend."

11 SPEAKING *Good intentions*

A **GROUP WORK** What are some things you would like to do in the future? Think of three intentions.

A: I'm going to learn how to sail.
B: That sounds fun. Are you going to take lessons?

B **CLASS ACTIVITY** Report the best intentions you heard. Then predict which ones will happen.

"Tatyana said she was going to learn how to sail, but she didn't want to take lessons."

12 INTERCHANGE 16 *Excuses, excuses*

Make some plans. Student A, go to Interchange 16A on page 129;
Student B, go to Interchange 16B on page 131.

The Truth About Lying

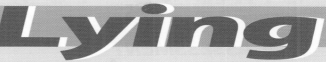

Is it ever better to tell a lie than the truth? If so, when?

Most of us are taught to believe that lying is wrong. But it seems that everybody tells lies – not big lies, but what we call "white lies." If we believe that lying is wrong, why do we do it? Most of the time, people have very good reasons for lying. For example, they might want to protect a friendship or someone's feelings. So, when do we lie and who do we lie to? A recent study found that the average person lies about seven times a day. Here are some reasons why.

1 **Lying to hide something:** People often lie because they want to hide something from someone. For example, a son doesn't tell his parents that he's dating a girl because he doesn't think

they will like her. Instead, he says he's going out with the guys.

2 **Lying to make an excuse:** Sometimes people lie because they don't want to do something. For example, someone invites you to a party. You think it will be boring, so you say you're busy.

3 **Lying to avoid sharing bad news:** Sometimes we don't want to tell someone bad news. For example, you have just had a very bad day at work, but you don't feel like talking about it. So if someone asks you about your day, you just say that everything was fine.

4 **Lying to make someone feel good:** Often we stretch the truth to make someone feel good. For example, your friend cooks dinner for you, but it tastes terrible. Do you say so? No. You probably say, "Mmm, this is delicious!"

A Read the article. Then complete the summary with information from the article.

It isn't necessarily .... to lie. It's probably OK to lie if you want to protect ....
or .... The main reasons for lying are to .... ,
to .... , to .... , or to ....

B Look at these situations. For each example, write the number of the appropriate reason.

.... 1. Your friend gives you an ugly shirt for your birthday. You say, "Oh, it's great!"
.... 2. Someone you don't like invites you to a movie, so you say, "I've already seen it."
.... 3. You lost your job and are having trouble finding a new one. When an old friend calls to find out how you are, you say you're doing well.
.... 4. You're planning a surprise party for a friend. To get him to come over at the right time, you ask him to stop by to see your new motorcycle.

C **GROUP WORK** Can you think of other reasons people tell white lies?
What white lies have you told recently?

Units 15–16 Progress check

SELF-ASSESSMENT

How well can you do these things? Check (✓) the boxes.

I can	Very well	OK	A little
Speculate about imaginary events (Ex. 1)	☐	☐	☐
Ask for and give advice and suggestions about past events (Ex. 2)	☐	☐	☐
Understand and report requests (Ex. 3)	☐	☐	☐
Report what people say (Ex. 4)	☐	☐	☐

 DISCUSSION *Interesting situations*

A What would you do in these situations? Complete the statements.

If I found a valuable piece of jewelry in the park, ...
If a friend gave me a present I didn't like, ...
If I wasn't invited to a party I wanted to attend, ...
If a classmate wanted to copy my homework, ...
If someone took my clothes while I was swimming, ...

B **GROUP WORK** Compare your responses. For each situation, choose one to tell the class.

A: What would you do if you found some jewelry in the park?
B: I'd probably keep it. You'd never be able to find the owner.

2 SPEAKING *Dilemmas*

A Make up two situations like the one below. Think about experiences you have had or heard about at work, home, or school.

"A friend visited me recently. We had a great time at first, but she became annoying. She borrowed my clothes and refused to pay for things. After two weeks, I told her she had to leave because my parents were coming."

B **PAIR WORK** Take turns sharing your situations. Ask for advice and suggestions.

A: What would you have done?
B: Well, I would have told her to leave after three days.

3 LISTENING *Take a message.*

A ▶ Listen to the conversations. Who would make these requests?
Match conversations 1 to 6 to the correct person.

.... a. boss   .... c. neighbor   .... e. classmate
.... b. doctor   .... d. parent   .... f. teacher

B ▶ Listen again. Complete the requests.

1. Please ....   4. Can .... ?
2. Can .... ?   5. Please ....
3. Don't ....   6. Please don't ....

C PAIR WORK Work with a partner. Imagine these requests were for you.
Take turns reporting the requests to your partner.

4 GAME *Tell the truth.*

A Think of situations when you expressed anger, gave an excuse, or
made a complaint. Write a brief statement about each situation.

> I once complained about the food in a restaurant.

B CLASS ACTIVITY Play a game. Choose three students to be contestants.

Step 1: The contestants compare their statements and choose one. This statement should be true
about only one student. The other two students should pretend they had the experience.

Step 2: The contestants stand in front of the class. Each contestant reads the same statement. The rest
of the class must ask questions to find out who isn't telling the truth.

> Contestant A, what restaurant were you in?

> Contestant B, what was wrong with the food?

> Contestant C, what did the waiter do?

Step 3: Who isn't telling the truth? What did he or she say to make you think that?

"I don't think Contestant A is telling the truth. He said he couldn't
remember the name of the restaurant!"

WHAT'S NEXT?

Look at your Self-assessment again. Do you need to review anything?

CONSIDER THE CONSEQUENCES

A Read over this questionnaire. Check (✓) the box for your opinion.

1 If people watch less TV, they'll talk more with their families.
- ☐ I agree.
- ☐ I don't agree.
- ☐ It depends.

2 If children watch a lot of violent programs on TV, they'll become violent themselves.
- ☐ I agree.
- ☐ I don't agree.
- ☐ It depends.

3 If people work only four days a week, their lives will improve.
- ☐ I agree.
- ☐ I don't agree.
- ☐ It depends.

4 If a child has brothers and sisters, he or she won't ever feel lonely or sad.
- ☐ I agree.
- ☐ I don't agree.
- ☐ It depends.

5 If a woman works outside the home, her children won't be happy.
- ☐ I agree.
- ☐ I don't agree.
- ☐ It depends.

6 If you have too many online friends, you'll have fewer "real" friends.
- ☐ I agree.
- ☐ I don't agree.
- ☐ It depends.

7 If the city lowers the cost of public transportation, more people will use it.
- ☐ I agree.
- ☐ I don't agree.
- ☐ It depends.

8 If there is a heavy fine for littering, our streets will be much cleaner.
- ☐ I agree.
- ☐ I don't agree.
- ☐ It depends.

9 If teachers put their class assignments on the Internet, students might see homework as a fun activity and enjoy doing it.
- ☐ I agree.
- ☐ I don't agree.
- ☐ It depends.

10 If teachers give harder tests, students will study harder for them.
- ☐ I agree.
- ☐ I don't agree.
- ☐ It depends.

B GROUP WORK Compare your opinions. Be prepared to give reasons for your opinions.

A: I think if people watch less TV, they'll talk more with their families.
B: I don't really agree.
C: Why not?
B: If they don't watch TV, they'll do something else.
They may spend all day on the computer.

A Look at the following job descriptions. Choose one job that you'd like to apply for.

JOB BOARD

| Find a job . . . ▶ | Post a job . . . ▶ |

Marketing Manager

Requirements:
• A business degree or marketing experience
• Able to travel and work long hours
• Enjoy sports and fitness activities

Responsibilities:
• Interviewing people about their sports preferences, writing reports, and working with famous athletes

Personal Assistant

Requirements:
• Excellent telephone skills
• Able to work flexible hours
• Able to take orders and make important decisions

Responsibilities:
• Maintaining the calendar of a busy celebrity, scheduling meetings, and preparing the star for public appearances

Activities Director

Requirements:
• Experience working with tourists
• A "people person"
• Outgoing and creative personality

Responsibilities:
• Organizing all leisure activities on a popular cruise ship, including planning daily tours, special menus, and nightly entertainment

---

B PAIR WORK Take turns interviewing each other for the job you each want. Give as much information as you can to show that you are the right person for the job.

C PAIR WORK Would you hire your partner for the job? Why or why not?

D PAIR WORK What is your dream job?

useful questions
What kind of degree do you have?
What work experience do you have?
What hours can you work?
Do you mind working . . . ?
Are you interested in working with . . . ?
Why should I hire you for the job?

WHO IS THIS BY?

A List one movie, one TV show, one song, and one book.

B **GROUP WORK** Take turns making a statement about each item. Does everyone agree with each statement?

A: *The Hobbit* was filmed in the United States.
B: Are you sure? Wasn't it filmed in Australia?
C: I'm pretty sure it was New Zealand.

C Now think of other famous creations and creators. Complete the chart. Make some of the items true and some of them false.

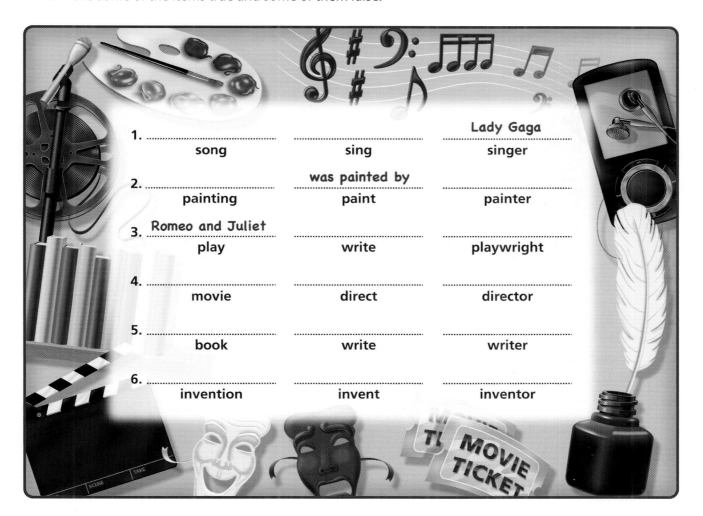

1.	....	Lady Gaga ....
song	sing	singer
2.	was painted by	....
painting	paint	painter
3. Romeo and Juliet	....	....
play	write	playwright
4.	....	....
movie	direct	director
5.	....	....
book	write	writer
6.	....	....
invention	invent	inventor

D **GROUP WORK** Make a statement about each item to your group members. Ask them to decide which statements are true and which are false.

A: The song "Bad Romance" was sung by Lady Gaga.
B: I think that's false.
C: No, that's true. I'm sure of it.

A **GROUP WORK** Play the board game. Follow these instructions.

1. Use small pieces of paper with your initials on them as markers.

2. Take turns by tossing a coin:

 Move two spaces.

Heads

Move one space.

Tails

3. Complete the sentence in the space you land on. Others ask two follow-up questions to get more information.

A: When I was little, I had a red bicycle.
B: Oh, really? Did you ride it every day?
A: No, I never rode it.
C: Why didn't you ever ride it?

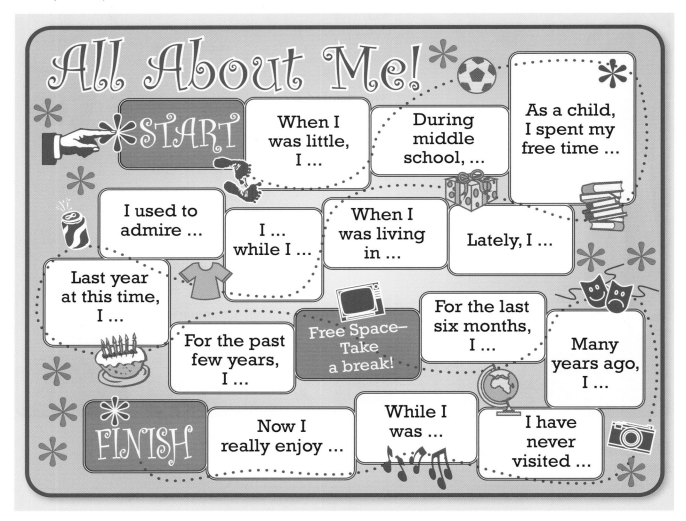

B **CLASS ACTIVITY** Tell the class an interesting fact that you learned about someone in your group.

"On his first day of middle school, Danny lost his backpack."

A Complete this questionnaire.

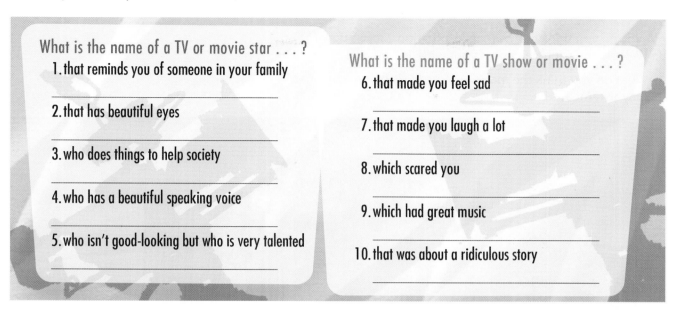

What is the name of a TV or movie star . . . ?
1. that reminds you of someone in your family
_____
2. that has beautiful eyes
_____
3. who does things to help society
_____
4. who has a beautiful speaking voice
_____
5. who isn't good-looking but who is very talented
_____

What is the name of a TV show or movie . . . ?
6. that made you feel sad
_____
7. that made you laugh a lot
_____
8. which scared you
_____
9. which had great music
_____
10. that was about a ridiculous story
_____

B **PAIR WORK** Compare your questionnaires. Ask follow-up questions of your own.

A: What is the name of a TV or movie star that reminds you of someone in your family?
B: Tom Cruise.
A: Who does he remind you of?
B: My brother, Todd.
A: Really? Why?
B: Because he looks like my brother. They have the same smile.

A PAIR WORK Look at this scene of a crowded restaurant. What do you think is happening in each of the five situations? Look at people's body language for clues.

A: Why do you think the woman in situation 2 looks upset?
B: Well, she might be having a fight with . . .

A: What do you think the man's gesture in situation 2 means?
B: Maybe it means he . . .

B GROUP WORK Compare your interpretations. Do you agree or disagree?

Student A

A **PAIR WORK** You and your partner want to get together. Ask and answer questions to find a day when you are both free. You also want to keep time open for other friends, so make up excuses for those days. Write your partner's excuses on the calendar.

A: Do you want to go out on the 2nd?
B: I'm sorry. I'm going to my friend's wedding. Are you free on the 1st?
A: Well, I . . .

B **PAIR WORK** Now work with another Student A. Discuss the excuses Student B gave you. Decide which excuses were probably true and which ones were probably not true.

A: Anna said that on the 9th she had to stay home and reorganize her clothes closet. That was probably not true.
B: I agree. I think . . .

A What would you do in each of these situations? Circle **a**, **b**, or **c**. If you think you would do something else, write your suggestion next to **d**.

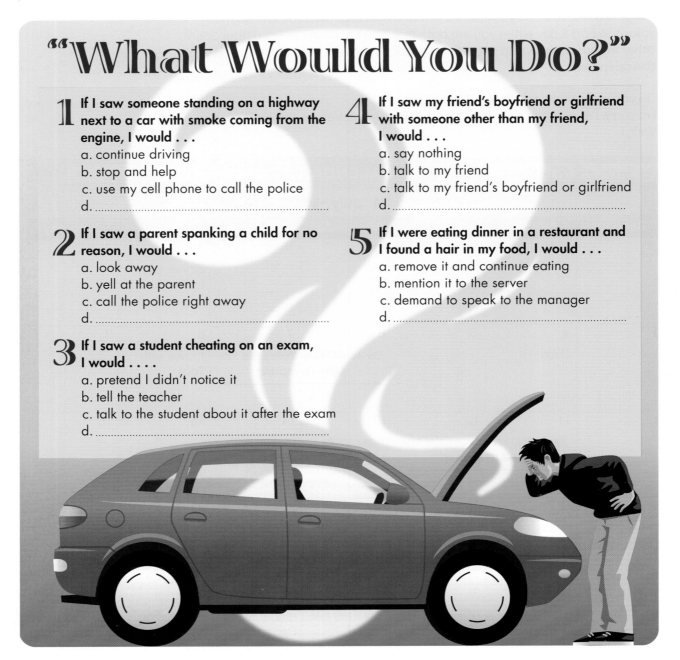

"What Would You Do?"

1 If I saw someone standing on a highway next to a car with smoke coming from the engine, I would . . .
a. continue driving
b. stop and help
c. use my cell phone to call the police
d. ....

2 If I saw a parent spanking a child for no reason, I would . . .
a. look away
b. yell at the parent
c. call the police right away
d. ....

3 If I saw a student cheating on an exam, I would . . . .
a. pretend I didn't notice it
b. tell the teacher
c. talk to the student about it after the exam
d. ....

4 If I saw my friend's boyfriend or girlfriend with someone other than my friend, I would . . .
a. say nothing
b. talk to my friend
c. talk to my friend's boyfriend or girlfriend
d. ....

5 If I were eating dinner in a restaurant and I found a hair in my food, I would . . .
a. remove it and continue eating
b. mention it to the server
c. demand to speak to the manager
d. ....

B **GROUP WORK** Compare your choices for each situation in part A.

A: What would you do if you saw someone standing on a highway next to a car with smoke coming from the engine?
B: Honestly, I would probably continue driving.
C: Really? I wouldn't. I would . . .

C **CLASS ACTIVITY** Take a class survey. Find out which choice was most popular for each situation. Talk about any other suggestions people added for **d**.

Student B

A PAIR WORK You and your partner want to get together. Ask and answer questions to find a day when you are both free. You also want to keep time open for other friends, so make up excuses for those days. Write your partner's excuses on the calendar.

A: Do you want to go out on the 2nd?
B: I'm sorry. I'm going to my friend's wedding. Are you free on the 1st?
A: Well, I . . .

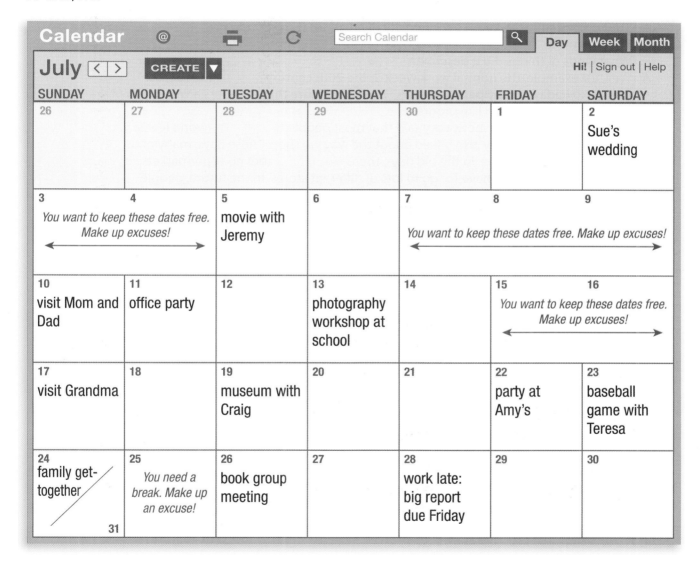

SUNDAY	MONDAY	TUESDAY	WEDNESDAY	THURSDAY	FRIDAY	SATURDAY
26	27	28	29	30	1	2 Sue's wedding
3	4	5 movie with Jeremy	6	7	8	9
You want to keep these dates free. Make up excuses! ←———————→				*You want to keep these dates free. Make up excuses!* ←———————————————→		
10 visit Mom and Dad	11 office party	12	13 photography workshop at school	14	15	16
					You want to keep these dates free. Make up excuses! ←———————————→	
17 visit Grandma	18	19 museum with Craig	20	21	22 party at Amy's	23 baseball game with Teresa
24 family get-together	25 *You need a break. Make up an excuse!*	26 book group meeting	27	28 work late: big report due Friday	29	30
31						

B PAIR WORK Now work with another Student B. Discuss the excuses Student A gave you. Decide which excuses were probably true and which ones were probably not true.

A: Joe said that on the 6th he had to stay home and reorganize his clothes closet. That was probably not true.
B: I agree. I think . . .

Grammar plus

Unit 9

1 Time contrasts (page 59)

> ▶ Use the modal *might* to say something is possible in the present or future: In a few years, movie theaters **might** not exist. = In a few years, maybe movie theaters won't exist.

Complete the conversation with the correct form of the verbs in parentheses. Use the past, present, or future tense.

A: I saw a fascinating program last night. It talked about the past, the present, and the future.

B: What kinds of things did it describe?

A: Well, for example, the normal work week in the 20th century .... (be) 35 hours. Nowadays, many people .... (work) more than 40 hours a week.

B: Well, that doesn't sound like progress.

A: You're right. But on the show, they said that most people .... (work) fewer hours in the future. They also talked about the way we shop. These days, many of us .... (shop) online. In the old days, there .... (be) no supermarkets, so people .... (have to) go to lots of different stores. In the future, people .... (do) all their shopping online.

B: I don't believe that.

A: Me neither. What about cars? Do you think people .... (still drive) cars a hundred years from now?

B: What did they say on the show?

A: They said that before the car, people .... (walk) everywhere. Nowadays, we .... (drive) everywhere. And that .... (not change).

2 Conditional sentences with *if* clauses (page 61)

> ▶ The *if* clause can come before or after the main clause: **If** I change my eating habits, I'll feel healthier. / I'll feel healthier **if** I change my eating habits. Always use a comma when the *if* clause comes before the main clause.
> ▶ For the future of *can*, use *will be able to*: If you save some money, you**'ll be able to buy** a car. (NOT: . . . you'll can buy a car.)
> ▶ For the future of *must*, use *will have to*: If you get a dog, you**'ll have to take care** of it. (NOT: . . . you'll must take care of it.)

Complete the sentences with the correct form of the verbs in parentheses.

1. If you ......*exercise*...... (exercise) more often, you ...*'ll feel*........... (feel) more energetic.
2. If you .... (join) a gym, exercise .... (become) part of your routine.
3. You .... (not have to) worry about staying in shape if you .... (work out) three or four times a week.
4. If you .... (ride) a bike or .... (run) a few times a week, you .... (lose) weight and .... (gain) muscle.
5. You .... (sleep) better at night if you .... (exercise) regularly.
6. If you .... (start) exercising, you .... (might/not have) as many colds and other health problems

Unit 10

1 Gerunds; short responses (page 65)

> Short responses with *so* and *neither* are ways of agreeing. The subject (noun or pronoun) comes after the verb: I love traveling. So **do I**. (NOT: So ~~I do.~~) I can't stand talking on the phone. Neither **can I**. (NOT: Neither ~~I can.~~)

Rewrite A's line using the words given. Then write an agreement for B.

1. I hate waiting in line at the bank. (can't stand)
   A: <u>I can't stand waiting in line at the bank.</u>
   B: <u>Neither can I.</u>
2. I don't like reading about politics or politicians. (interested in)
   A: ....
   B: ....
3. I can remember people's names. (good at)
   A: ....
   B: ....
4. I have no problem with working on weekends. (don't mind)
   A: ....
   B: ....
5. I love going for long walks in my free time. (enjoy)
   A: ....
   B: ....
6. I can't manage time well. (not good at)
   A: ....
   B: ....

2 Clauses with *because* (page 68)

> Clauses with *because* answer the question "Why?" or "Why not?": Why would you make a good flight attendant? I'd make a good flight attendant **because** I love traveling and I'm good with people.

Complete the sentences with *because* and the phrases in the box.

```
   I don't write very well
   I love arguing with people
   I'm afraid of flying
✓  I'm much too short
   I'm not patient enough to work with kids
   I'm really bad with numbers
```

1. I could never be a fashion model <u>because I'm much too short.</u>
2. I wouldn't make a good high school teacher ....
3. I wouldn't want to be a flight attendant ....
4. I could never be an accountant ....
5. I would make a bad journalist ....
6. I'd be an excellent lawyer ....

Unit 11

1 Passive with *by* (simple past) (page 73)

▶ The past participle of regular verbs is the same form as the simple past: Leonardo da Vinci **painted** *Mona Lisa* in 1503. *Mona Lisa* was **painted** by Leonardo da Vinci in 1503.

▶ The past participle of some – but not all – irregular verbs is the same form as the simple past: The Egyptians **built** the Pyramids. The Pyramids were **built** by the Egyptians. BUT Jane Austen **wrote** *Pride and Prejudice*. *Pride and Prejudice* was **written** by Jane Austen.

Change the sentences from active to passive with *by*.

1. The Chinese invented paper around 100 C.E.
   Paper was invented by the Chinese around 100 C.E.
2. Marie Curie discovered radium in 1898.
   ....
3. Dr. Felix Hoffmann made the first aspirin in 1899.
   ....
4. Tim Berners-Lee developed the World Wide Web in 1989.
   ....
5. William Herschel identified the planet Uranus in 1781.
   ....
6. Georges Bizet wrote the opera *Carmen* in the 1870s.
   ....

2 Passive without *by* (simple present) (page 75)

▶ When it is obvious or not important who is doing the action, don't use a *by* phrase: Both the Olympics and the World Cup are held every four years. (NOT: . . . are held ~~by people~~ . . .)

Complete the information with *is* or *are* and the past participle of the verbs in the box.

| base |
| export |
| import |
| know |
| ✓ speak |
| use |

1. Portuguese – not Spanish – ......*is spoken*...... in Brazil.
2. Diamonds and gold from South Africa .... by countries all over the world.
3. The U.S. dollar .... in Puerto Rico.
4. Hawaii .... for its beautiful beaches.
5. Many electronic products .... by Japan and Korea. It's an important industry for these two countries.
6. The economy in many island countries, such as Jamaica, ... on tourism.

Unit 12

1 Past continuous vs. simple past (page 79)

▶ When the past continuous is used with the simple past, both actions happened at the same time but the past continuous action started earlier. The simple past action interrupted the past continuous action.

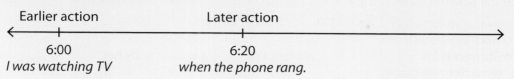

Earlier action   Later action

6:00   6:20
I was watching TV   *when the phone rang.*

Complete the conversations with the correct form of the verbs in parentheses. Use the past continuous or the simple past.

1. A: What happened to you?
   B: I ....*fell*............ (fall) while I .....*was jogging*..... (jog) in the park.
2. A: .... you .... (see) the storm yesterday?
   B: Yes. It .... (start) while I .... (drive) to work.
3. A: We finally .... (move) to a larger apartment.
   B: That's good. I know you .... (live) in a tiny place when your daughter .... (be) born.
4. A: My sister .... (have) a bad accident. She .... (hurt) her back when she .... (lift) weights at the gym.
   B: That .... (happen) to me last year, but I .... (not lift) weights. I .... (take) a boxing class and I .... (trip).

2 Present perfect continuous (page 81)

▶ The same time expressions used with the present perfect can also be used with the present perfect continuous. Don't confuse *for* and *since*: I've been working here **for** five years./I've been working here **since** 2010.

Complete the sentences with the present perfect continuous form of the verbs in parentheses.

1. A: What ....*have*............ you .....*been doing*..... all day?
   B: I .... (clean) the house, and Peter .... (watch) TV. He .... (not feel) very well lately.
   A: How .... you .... (feel) these days?
   B: I .... (feel) great. I .... (not eat) any junk food, and I .... (exercise) a lot. I .... (take) really good care of myself.
2. A: How long .... you and Joe .... (date)?
   B: We .... (go out) together for almost a year. Can you believe it?
   A: Maya and I .... (date) for even longer. I think it's time to get married. We .... (talk) about it a lot lately.
   B: Joe and I .... (not talk) about marriage, but I .... (think) about it.

Unit 13

1 Participles as adjectives (page 87)

▶ Adjectives ending in –ing are present participles. They are things that *cause* a feeling. Adjectives ending in –ed are past participles. They *express* the feeling.

Complete the sentences with the correct participle.

1. Why are we watching this ....*boring*........ movie? Are you ....*bored*.......... with it? (boring/bored)
2. Kristen Stewart is an .... actress. I'm .... by her talent. (amazing/amazed)
3. Are you .... in computer-generated special effects? The latest 3-D movies are very .... (interesting/interested)
4. I had an .... experience the last time I went to the movies. I started to cough, and I couldn't stop. I was really .... (embarrassing/embarrassed)
5. Julie and I saw the new *Pirates of the Caribbean* movie. I found it .... , but Julie didn't seem very .... by it. (amusing/amused)
6. Oh, I'm really .... with Jeremy right now. He took me to the most .... movie last night. I wanted to walk out after half an hour, but he wouldn't leave! (disgusting/disgusted)
7. Do you think sci-fi movie directors make their films .... intentionally? I get so .... by the complicated storylines and weird characters. (confusing/confused)
8. I think that great books make great movies. If I find a book .... , I'm usually .... by the movie also. (fascinating/fascinated)

2 Relative pronouns for people and things (page 89)

▶ Relative clauses give information about nouns. Don't use a personal pronoun in a relative clause: He's an actor **that** won two Oscars. (NOT: He's an actor that ~~he~~ won two Oscars.)

Complete the conversations. Use *that* for things and *who* for people.

A: How did you like the movie last night? Was it any good?
B: It wasn't bad, but it's not the kind of movie ......*that*...... makes you think. I like films .... have a strong message and interesting storylines.
A: How about the acting? Did you like the actors .... star in it?
B: Cameron Diaz is pretty good, actually.
A: Oh, she's the blonde actress .... was going out with Justin Timberlake.
B: Justin who? Who's that?
A: Oh, you know him. He's the one .... was in the band 'N Sync years ago. It was a "boy band" .... was popular in the 1990s.
B: I remember 'N Sync, but I don't remember the names of the guys .... were in the band.
A: Well, I loved Justin Timberlake when I was a kid. And he's not a bad actor. Did you see the movie *The Social Network*?
B: I did see that. It's about the guys .... started Facebook, right? I didn't realize Justin Timberlake was in it. Now I'll have to see it again!

Unit 14

1 Modals and adverbs (page 93)

▶ Use the modals *might/may, could,* and *must* and the adverbs *maybe/perhaps,*
possibly/probably, and *definitely* when you aren't sure about what you're saying:
slight possibility: *might, may, maybe, perhaps*
possibility: *could, possibly, probably*
strong possibility: *must, definitely*

Rewrite each sentence in different ways, using the words in parentheses.

1. Perhaps it means she doesn't agree with you.
   a. (maybe) Maybe it means she doesn't agree with you.
   b. (might) ....
   c. (may) ....
2. That gesture could mean "Come here."
   a. (possibly) ....
   b. (probably) ....
3. That almost definitely means he doesn't understand you.
   a. (must) ....

2 Permission, obligation, and prohibition (page 95)

▶ Use *have/has* with *got to*: You**'ve got to** keep the door closed. (NOT: You ~~got to~~ keep
the door closed.)

Complete the conversations with the words and phrases in the box. Use each word
or phrase only once.

> are allowed to
> aren't allowed to
> can
> ✓ can't
> have to
> have got to

1. A: Oh, no! That sign says "No fishing." That means we ....can't..........
   fish here.
   B: You're right. We .... go somewhere else to fish. I think
      you .... fish in the pond on Cedar Road. Let's go there.
2. A: What does that sign mean?
   B: It means bad news for us. It means you .... bring dogs
      to the beach. We'd better take Buddy home.
3. A: Please don't leave your garbage here. You .... put it in
      the trash room down the hall. That's one of the building's rules.
   B: I'm really sorry.
4. A: You .... put your bike in the bike room downstairs, if
      you want. It's much safer than locking it up outside.
   B: Oh, that's great! I'll do that. I didn't know about the bike room.

Unit 15

1 Unreal conditional sentences with *if* clauses (page 101)

▶ The clauses in unreal conditional sentences can come in either order. Don't use a comma when the *if* clause comes second: **If** I won the lottery, I'd share the money with my family./I'd share the money with my family **if** I won the lottery.

Complete the conversation with the correct form of the verbs in parentheses.

1. A: If a friend ....*asked*.......... (ask) to borrow some money, what .....*would*..... you ......*say*...... (say)?
   B: Well, if I .... (have) any extra money that month, I .... probably .... (give) it to her.

2. A: What .... you .... (do) if someone .... (give) you a million dollars?
   B: Hmm, I'm not sure. I .... (buy) a lot of nice clothes and jewelry, or I .... (spend) some and .... (give) some away, or I .... (put) it all in the bank.

3. A: If you .... (think) a friend was doing something dangerous, ... you .... (say) something to him, or .... you .... (keep) quiet?
   B: I .... definitely .... (talk) to my friend about it.

4. A: What .... you .... (do) if you .... (have) a problem with your boss?
   B: That's a hard one. If that .... (happen), I .... (talk) to the Human Resources department about it, or I .... just .... (sit down) with my boss and .... (talk) about the situation.

2 Past modals (page 103)

▶ Use *should have* and *would have* for all subjects. They don't change form: He **should have called** sooner. (NOT: He should ~~has~~ called sooner.)

Read the situations. Use the words in parentheses to write opinions and suggestions.

1. My neighbor had a party last night. It was very loud, so I called the police.
   (you / speak / to your neighbor first)
   You should have spoken to your neighbor first...

2. The mail carrier put someone else's mail in my box. I threw it away.
   (you / write / a note and leave / the mail in your box)

   ....

3. My sister asked if I liked her new dress. It didn't look good on her, but I said it did. (I / tell her the truth)

   ....

4. A salesperson called me last night. I didn't want to buy anything, but I let her talk to me for almost half an hour.
   (I / tell her I'm not interested / hang up)

   ....

Unit 16

1 Reported speech: requests (page 107)

▶ When a reported request is negative, *not* comes before *to*: Don't leave your wet towel on the floor. She told me **not to leave** my wet towel on the floor. (NOT: She told me ~~to not~~ leave my wet towel on the floor.)

Harry's roommate, Tyler, is making some requests. Read what Tyler said to Harry. Write the requests with the verb in parentheses and reported speech.

1. "Can you put away your clean clothes?" (ask)
   Tyler asked Harry to put away his clean clothes.
2. "Meet me in the cafeteria at school at noon." (say)
   ....
3. "Don't leave your shoes in the living room." (tell)
   ....
4. "Hang up your wet towels." (say)
   ....
5. "Could you stop using my phone?" (ask)
   ....
6. "Make your bed on weekdays." (tell)
   ....
7. "Don't eat my food." (say)
   ....
8. "Be a better roommate!" (tell)
   ....

2 Reported speech: statements (page 109)

▶ The tense of the introducing verb (*ask, say, tell*) changes when the sentence is reported: simple present → simple past; present continuous → past continuous; present perfect → past perfect. Modals change, too: *can* → *could*; *will* → *would*; *may* → *might*.

Bill and Kathy are having a barbecue on Sunday. They're upset because a lot of their friends can't come. Read what their friends said. Change the excuses into reported speech.

1. Lori: "I have to visit my grandparents that day."
   Lori said that she had to visit her grandparents that day.
2. Mario: "I'm going to a play on Sunday."
   ....
3. Julia: "I've promised to take my brother to the movies that day."
   ....
4. Daniel: "I can't come. I have to study for a huge exam on Monday."
   ....
5. The neighbors: "We'll be out of town all weekend."
   ....
6. Alice: "I may have to babysit my nephew."
   ....

Grammar plus answer key

Unit 9

1 Time contrasts

A: Well, for example, the normal work week in the 20th century **was** 35 hours. Nowadays, many people **work/are working** more than 40 hours a week.

B: Well, that doesn't sound like progress.

A: You're right. On the show, they said that most people **will work/might work** fewer hours in the future. They also talked about the way we shop. These days, many of us **shop** online. In the old days, there **were** no supermarkets, so people **had to/ used to have to go** to lots of different stores. In the future, people **will do/are going to do** all their shopping online.

B: I don't believe that.

A: Me neither. What about cars? Do you think people **will still drive/are still going to drive** cars a hundred years from now?

B: What did they say on the show?

A: They said that before the car, people **used to walk/walked** everywhere. Nowadays, we drive everywhere. And that **isn't going to change/'s not going to change/won't change**.

2 Conditional sentences with *if* clauses

2. join / will become
3. won't have to / work out
4. ride / run / you'll lose / gain
5. You'll sleep / exercise
6. start / might not have

Unit 10

1 Gerunds; short responses

2. A: I'm not interested in reading about politics or politicians.
   B: Neither am I.
3. A: I'm good at remembering people's names.
   B: So am I.
4. A: I don't mind working on weekends.
   B: Neither do I.
5. A: I enjoy going for long walks in my free time.
   B: So do I.
6. A: I'm not good at managing time well.
   B: Neither am I.

2 Clauses with *because*

2. I wouldn't make a good high school teacher **because I'm not patient enough to work with kids.**
3. I wouldn't want to be a flight attendant **because I'm afraid of flying.**
4. I could never be an accountant **because I'm really bad with numbers.**
5. I would make a bad journalist **because I don't write very well.**
6. I'd be an excellent lawyer **because I love arguing with people.**

Unit 11

1 Passive with *by* (simple past)

2. Radium was discovered by Marie Curie in 1898.

3. The first aspirin was made by Dr. Felix Hoffmann in 1899.
4. The World Wide Web was developed by Tim Berners-Lee in 1989.
5. The planet Uranus was identified in 1781 by William Herschel.
6. The opera *Carmen* was written by Georges Bizet in the 1870s.

2 Passive without *by* (simple present)

2. Diamonds and gold from South Africa **are imported** by countries all over the world.
3. The U.S. dollar **is used** in Puerto Rico.
4. Hawaii **is known** for its beautiful beaches.
5. Many electronic products **are exported** by Japan and Korea. It's an important industry for these two countries.
6. The economy in many island countries, such as Jamaica, **is based** on tourism.

Unit 12

1 Past continuous vs. simple past

2. A: **Did** you **see** the storm yesterday?
   B: Yes! It **started** while I **was driving** to work.
3. A: We finally **moved** to a larger apartment.
   B: That's good. I know you **were living** in a tiny place when your daughter **was** born.
4. A: My sister **had** a bad accident. She **hurt** her back when she **was lifting** weights at the gym.
   B: That **happened** to me last year, but I **wasn't lifting** weights. I **was taking** a boxing class and I **tripped**.

2 Present perfect continuous

1. A: What **have** you **been doing** all day?
   B: I**'ve been cleaning** the house, and Peter **has been watching** TV. He **hasn't been feeling** very well lately.
   A: How **have** you **been feeling** these days?
   B: I**'ve been feeling** great. I **haven't been eating** any junk food, and I**'ve been exercising** a lot. I**'ve been taking** really good care of myself.
2. A: How long **have** you and Joe **been dating**?
   B: We**'ve been going out** together for almost a year. Can you believe it?
   A: Maya and I **have been dating** for even longer. I think it's time to get married. We**'ve been talking** about it a lot lately.
   B: Joe and I **haven't been talking** about marriage, but I**'ve been thinking** about it.

Unit 13

1 Participles as adjectives

2. Kristen Stewart is an **amazing** actress. I'm **amazed** by her talent.
3. Are you **interested** in computer-generated special effects? The latest 3D movies are very **interesting**.

4. I had an **embarrassing** experience the last time I went to the movies. I started to cough, and I couldn't stop. I was really **embarrassed**.
5. Julie and I saw the new *Pirates of the Caribbean* movie. I found it **amusing**, but Julie didn't seem very **amused** by it.
6. Oh, I'm really **disgusted** with Jeremy right now. He took me to the most **disgusting** movie last night. I wanted to walk out after half an hour, but he wouldn't leave!
7. Do you think sci-fi movie directors make their films **confusing** intentionally? I get so **confused** by the complicated storylines and weird characters.
8. I think that great books make great movies. If I find a book **fascinating**, I'm usually **fascinated** by the movie also.

2 Relative clauses for people and things

A: How did you like the movie last night? Was it any good?
B: It wasn't bad, but it's not the kind of movie **that** makes you think. I like films **that** have a strong message and interesting storylines.
A: How about the acting? Did you like the actors **who** star in it?
B: Cameron Diaz is pretty good, actually.
A: Oh, she's the blonde actress **who** was going out with Justin Timberlake.
B: Justin who? Who's that?
A: Oh, you know him. He's the one **who** was in the band 'N Sync years ago. It was a "boy band" **that** was popular in the 1990s.
B: I remember 'N Sync, but I don't remember the names of the guys **who** were in the band.
A: Well, I loved Justin Timberlake when I was a kid. And he's not a bad actor. Did you see the movie *The Social Network*?
B: I did see that. It's about the guys **who** started Facebook, right? I didn't realize Justin Timberlake was in it. Now I'll have to see it again!

Unit 14

1 Modals and adverbs

1. a. Maybe it means she doesn't agree with you.
   b. It might mean she doesn't agree with you.
   c. It may mean she doesn't agree with you.
2. a. That gesture possibly means "Come here."
   b. That gesture probably means "Come here."
3. a. That must mean he doesn't understand you.

2 Permission, obligation, and prohibition

1. A: Oh, no! That sign says "No fishing." That means we **can't** fish here.
   B: You're right. We**'ve got to/have to** go somewhere else to fish. I think **you're allowed to/can** fish in the pond on Cedar Road. Let's go there.
2. A: What does that sign mean?
   B: It means bad news for us. It means you **aren't allowed to** bring dogs to the beach. We'd better take Buddy home.
3. A: Please don't leave your garbage here. You**'ve got to/have to** put it in the trash room down the hall. That's one of the building's rules.
   B: I'm really sorry.

4. A: You **can** put your bike in the bike room downstairs, if you want. It's much safer than locking it up outside.
   B: Oh, that's great! I'll do that. I didn't know about the bike room.

Unit 15

1 Unreal conditional sentences with *if*

1. A: If a friend **asked** to borrow some money, what **would** you **say**?
   B: Well, if I **had** any extra money that month, I **would** probably **give** it to her.
2. A: What **would/could** you **do** if someone **gave** you a million dollars?
   B: Hmm, I'm not sure. I **could/might buy** a lot of nice clothes and jewelry, or I **could/might spend** some and **give** some away, or I **could/might put** it all in the bank.
3. A: If you **thought** a friend was doing something dangerous, **would** you **say** something to him, or **would** you **keep** quiet?
   B: I **would** definitely **talk** to my friend about it.
4. A: What **would** you **do** if you **had** a problem with your boss?
   B: That's a hard one. If that **happened**, I **might talk** to the Human Resources department about it, or I **might/could** just **sit down** with my boss and **talk** about the situation.

2 Past modals

2. You should have written a note and left the mail in your box.
3. I would have told her the truth.
4. I would have told her I wasn't interested and hung up (the phone).

Unit 16

1 Reported speech: requests

2. Tyler said to meet him in the cafeteria at school at noon.
3. Tyler told him/Harry not to leave his shoes in the living room.
4. Tyler said to hang up his wet towels.
5. Tyler asked him/Harry to stop using his/Tyler's phone.
6. Tyler told him/Harry to make his bed on weekdays.
7. Tyler said not to eat his/Tyler's food.
8. Tyler told him/Harry to be a better roommate.

2 Reported speech: statements

1. Lori said (that) she had to visit her grandparents that day.
   Lori told them (that) she had to visit her grandparents that day.
2. Mario said/told them (that) he was going to a play on Sunday.
3. Julia said/told them (that) she had promised to take her brother to the movies that day.
4. Daniel said/told them (that) he couldn't come because he had to study for a huge exam on Monday.
5. The neighbors said/told them (that) they would be out of town all weekend.
6. Alice said/told them (that) she might have to babysit her nephew.

Credits

Illustrations

Andrezzinho: 16 (*top*), 43 (*top*), 62; **Ilias Arahovitis:** 37; **Mark Collins:** v, 16 (*bottom*), 36 (*top*), 41, 67 (*top*); **Carlos Diaz:** 39, 46, 93 (*bottom*), 104 (*center*), 114; **Jada Fitch:** 65, 119; **Travis Foster:** 20, 40 (*top*), 90 (*top*), 97 (*center*), 116 (*bottom*); **Chuck Gonzales:** 2, 30 (*bottom*), 64 (*bottom*), 106, 117; **Jim Haynes:** 36 (*bottom*), 75, 79, 99; **Trevor Keen:** 38, 61, 102, 121; **Jim Kelly:** 95 (*bottom earbuds, cell phone*) ; **Joanna Kerr:** 123; **KJA-artists:** 124 (*bottom*), 130; **Shelton Leong:** 22 (*bottom*), 58 (*bottom*), 108, 109; **Karen Minot:** 25 (*top*), 27, 32, 64 (*top*), 68, 72 (*top*), 76, 78, 90 (*bottom*), 105, 118, 129, 131; **Rob Schuster:** 8, 13, 18, 35, 40 (*bottom*), 44 (*early smartphone*), 50, 58 (*top*), 67 (*bottom*), 77, 86, 97, 122, 125; **Daniel Vasconcellos:** 15, 82, 110, 112; **Brad Walker:** 81, 100 (*bottom*); **Sam Whitehead:** 5, 6, 33, 43 (*bottom*), 53, 54, 92 (*bottom*), 93 (*top*), 127; **Jeff Wong:** 60; **James Yamasaki:** 19, 25 (*bottom*), 80, 94, 111; 128; **Rose Zgodzinski:** 2, 10, 22 (*top*), 30 (*top*), 44 (*top*), 55, 69, 78 (*top*), 92 (*top*), 120, 124 (*top*); **Carol Zuber-Mallison:** 7, 21, 26, 44 (*bottom*), 49, 63, 83, 85, 91, 100 (*top*), 104 (*bottom*), 116 (*top*), 126

Photos

2 (*left*) © Leslie Banks/iStockphoto; (*right*) © Jacqueline Veissid/Lifesize/Getty Images
3 © MIXA/Getty Images
6 © Stretch Photography/Blend Images/age fotostock
7 (*clockwise from top*) © Steve Granitz/WireImage/Getty Images; © MGM Studios/Moviepix/Getty Images; © Photos 12/Alamy
8 (*top middle*) © Ilene MacDonald/Alamy; (*top right*) © Temmuz Can Arsiray/iStockphoto; (*bottom, clockwise from left*) © Jeff Morgan 09/Alamy; © Peter Treanor/Alamy; © Daniel Borzynski/Alamy
9 © B. O'Kane/Alamy
11 © Zero Creatives/Cultura/Getty Images
13 (*top row*) © AP Photo/Uwe Lein; © AP Photo/Kydpl Kyodo; © Andrew Robinson/Alamy; © Courtesy of Wheelman Inc.
14 © Superstock/Getty Images
17 (*left to right*) © Imagemore Co. Ltd./Getty Images; © Niels Poulsen Mus/Alamy
18 © Yusuke Nakanishi/Aflo Foto Agency/Alamy
19 © Creatas/Punchstock
21 © Image100/age fotostock
22 (*top row*) © Topic Photo Agency/age fotostock; © Nico Tondini/age fotostock; © Eising/Bon Appetit/Alamy; © JTB Photo/SuperStock
23 © Juice Images/Alamy
24 (*top right*) © Jupiter Images/Foodpix/Getty Images; (*middle row*) © iStockphoto/Thinkstock; © Dave King/Dorling Kindersley/Getty Images; © Olga Utlyakova/iStockphoto; © funkyfood London-Paul Williams/Alamy; © John Kelly/Food Image Source/StockFood; © Eiichi Onodera/Getty Images
25 (*top left*) © Archive Photos/Stringer/Getty Images; (*middle row*) © George Kerrigan
26 (*top row*) © Shipes/Shooter/StockFood; © Olivier Blondeau/iStockphoto; © Brent Melton/iStockphoto; © Boris Ryzhkov/iStockphoto; © Morten Olsen/iStockphoto; (*middle right*) © Asiaselects/Getty Images; (*bottom right*) © Debbi Smirnoff/iStockphoto
27 (*top right*) © Altrendo/Getty Images; (*middle right*) © Sean Justice/Getty Images
29 (*middle right*) © Jiri Hera/Shutterstock; (*bottom right*) © AP Photo/Shizuo Kambayashi
30 (*top row*) © Travelscape Images/Alamy; © Chicasso/Blend Images; © i love images/Veer; © Larry Williams/LWA/Blend Images/Alamy
31 © Julien Capmeil/Photonica/Getty Images
34 (*middle right*) © Irene Alastruey/age fotostock; (*bottom left*) © Teresa Kasprzycka/Shutterstock
35 © Jeff Greenberg/Alamy
38 © UpperCut Images/Getty Images
42 © Tyler Stableford/Stone/Getty Images
44 (*clockwise from left*) © Jowita Stachowiak/iStockphoto; © SSPL/Getty Images; © RubberBall/Alamy; © David J. Green-studio/Alamy; © iStockphoto/Thinkstock; © Suto Norbert Zsolt/Shutterstock; © 7505811966/Shutterstock; © Oleksiy Mark/Shutterstock
45 (*top right*) © Mark Evans/iStockphoto; (*middle right*) © Schiller/F1online digitale Bildagentur GmbH/Alamy
46 © Sullivan/Corbis
47 (*top right*) © Jupiterimages/Comstock Images/Getty Images; (*bottom right, top to bottom*) © Miles Boyer/Shutterstock; © Mark Evans/iStockphoto; © broker/Veer
48 (*top row*) © mbbirdy/iStockphoto; © Maxim Pavlov/Veer; © Scanrail/Fotolia; © gabyjalbert/iStockphoto; © Christophe Testi/Shutterstock; (*bottom right*) © Monashee Frantz/Ojo Images/age fotostock
49 (*right, top to bottom*) © Jurgen Wiesler/Imagebroker/Alamy; © Alfaguarilla/Shutterstock

50 (*top row*) © Roberto Gerometta/Lonely Planet Images/Getty Images; © David Hancock/Alamy; © Toru Yamanaka/AFP/Getty Images; © Tipograffias/Shutterstock
51 (*clockwise from top*) © Michael Flippo/Fotolia; © Olga Lyubkina/iStockphoto; © DNY59/iStockphoto
52 (*top left*) © Masterfile; (*middle*) © AP Photo/Ibrahim Usta; (*middle right*) © Jack Hollingsworth/Asia Images//age fotostock; (*bottom right*) © Andy Chen/Flickr/Getty Images
53 © Christian Kober/AWL Images /Getty Images
55 (*top left*) © AP Photo/Collin Reid; (*top right*) © Michel Setboun/Corbis; (*middle left*) © Mickael David/Author's Image Ltd/Alamy; (*middle right*) © Ville Myllynen/AFP/Getty Images/NEWSCOM
56 © iStockphoto/Thinkstock
57 © Esbin Anderson/Photo Network/Alamy
58 (*top row*) © FPG/Retrofile/Getty Images; © Ariel Skelley/Blend Images/Corbis; © Colin Anderson/Blend Images/Corbis
59 © Evening Standard/Stringer/Hulton Archive /Getty Images
60 © Engine Images/Fotolia
63 © Lane Oatey/Getty Images
67 (*bottom row*) © PBNJ Productions/Blend Images/Getty Images; © imagebroker.net/SuperStock; © Joe McBride/Stone/Getty Images
69 © Peter Dazeley/Photographer's Choice/Getty Images
71 (*middle row*) © Peter Dazeley/The Image Bank/Getty Images; © Topic Photo Agency/age fotostock; © Digital Vision/Photodisc/Thinkstock
72 (*top row*) © Dinodia/age fotostock; © Angelo Cavalli/age fotostock; © Jean-Paul Azam/The Image Bank/Getty Images; © Siegfried Layda/Photographer's Choice/Getty Images; © Renault Philippe/Hemis/Alamy; (*bottom right*) © Mathias Beinling/Alamy
73 © Javier Soriano/AFP/Getty Images
74 (*middle row*) © iStockphoto/Thinkstock; © Takashi Katahira/Amana Images/Corbis; © Keren Su/Corbis
76 (*right, top to bottom*) © Mardagada/Alamy; © Timothy Fadek/Corbis; (*bottom right*) © Jim Holmes/Axiom Photographic Agency/Getty Images
77 (*top row*) © Yvette Cardozo/Alamy; © Robert Harding Picture Library/SuperStock; © Oliver Berg/epa/Corbis
78 (*top row*) © Jeff Sarpa/StockFood Creative/Getty Images; © Stocksnapper/Alamy; © Pando Hall/Photographer's Choice/Getty Images; (*bottom left*) © Cultura Creative/Alamy
80 © AP Photo/Xie zhengyi/Imaginechina
83 (*top right*) © La Belle Kinoise/AFP/Getty Images/NEWSCOM; (*middle left*) © Urman Lionel/SIPA/NEWSCOM
84 © 20th Century Fox Film Corp./Everett Collection
86 (*left, to bottom*) © AF archive/Alamy; © 20th Century Fox Film Corp./Everett Collection; (*right, top to bottom*) © AP Photo/Murray Close; © 20th Century Fox Film Corp./Everett Collection; (*bottom right*) © Mario Anzuoni/Reuters/Corbis
87 © Vera Anderson/WireImage/Getty Images
89 © Razorpix/Alamy
90 © David James/Twentieth Century Fox/Everett Collection
91 © Richard Foreman/Twentieth Century Fox Film Corp./Photofest
104 © Design Pics/Punchstock
107 © Photodisc/Getty Images
115 (*all*) (*Rio de Janeiro*) © John Banagan/age fotostock; (*Cairo*) © Robin Laurance/Look/age fotostock; (*Hong Kong*) © Martyn Vickery/Alamy; (*Salzburg*) © Lebrecht Music and Arts Photo Library/Alamy
118 © H.Mark Weidman Photography/Alamy
120 © Corbis flirt/Alamy
122 (*bottom row*) © Creatas Images/Thinkstock; © Chan Leong Hin/age fotostock; © Jay Newman/LWA/Blend Images/Getty Images
126 (*Heads, Tails*) © Jeffrey Kuan/iStockphoto

interchange

Jack C. Richards
Revised by Lynne Robertson

VIDEO ACTIVITY WORKSHEETS 2B

CAMBRIDGE
UNIVERSITY PRESS

Credits

Plan of Video 2B

Car, bike, or bus?

≣ Preview

1 CULTURE

The first vehicle similar to a bicycle was built in 1690 in France. It was called a hobbyhorse. In Scotland, in 1840, pedals were added and it became the first real bicycle. Today there are twice as many bicycles as cars. There are over a billion bicycles in the world, with 400 million of them in China alone. In the U.S., almost 90 universities now have a campus bike program. Students "check out" the bikes to get around campus. This helps cut down on traffic, reduce pollution, and improve campus safety, but students need to remember: The bikes still need to be locked!

Do people ride bicycles in your country? How about 25 years ago?
How do people travel now?
Do most people own a car? How about a bicycle?

2 VOCABULARY *Transportation costs*

A **PAIR WORK** Do you know all of these words? Circle the word in each item that doesn't belong.

1. car   insurance   parking ticket   ~~sidewalk~~
2. tires   expense   bicycle   helmet
3. job   loan   credit   debt
4. repairs   bus   route   public transportation
5. lend   commute   borrow   manage

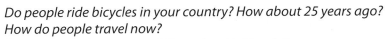

B Now choose two words from each item and use them in a sentence, like this:

"I bought a new car, but then I couldn't afford the insurance!"

3 GUESS THE STORY

Look at the characters. Which form of transportation do you think each one prefers? Write it on the line.

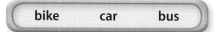

| bike | car | bus |

1. Luis   2. Jessica   3. Will   4. Emi

....

Watch the video

4 GET THE PICTURE

A Look at your answers to Exercise 3. Did you guess correctly? Write the transportation each person prefers in the chart.

	Luis	Jessica	Will	Emi
Transportation:	car			
Other:	can take out a car loan			

B Now write one more piece of information about each person. Compare with a partner.

5 WATCH FOR DETAILS

Check (✓) **True** or **False**. Then correct the false statements. Compare with a partner.

	True	False	
1. Luis rides a bike now.	☐	✔	Luis takes the bus now.
2. Luis has already told his wife about the car.	☐	☐	
3. Will rode his bike through a puddle.	☐	☐	
4. Jessica will drive to work after graduation.	☐	☐	
5. A car loan can help someone establish credit.	☐	☐	
6. Someone else bought the car Luis wants.	☐	☐	

6 WHAT'S YOUR OPINION?

A Complete the sentences with the consequences you think will happen.

1. If you buy a car before you have a job, ...
2. If you take out a car loan, ...
3. If you ride a bike instead of driving, ...
4. If you take the bus to work, ...
5. If you walk everywhere you go, ...
6. If you're not careful where you park your car, ...

B **PAIR WORK** Choose three sentences from part A and share your opinions.

Follow-up

7 YOUR CITY

A **PAIR WORK** In your city or town, what are the advantages and disadvantages of these forms of transportation? Complete the chart. Then compare around the class.

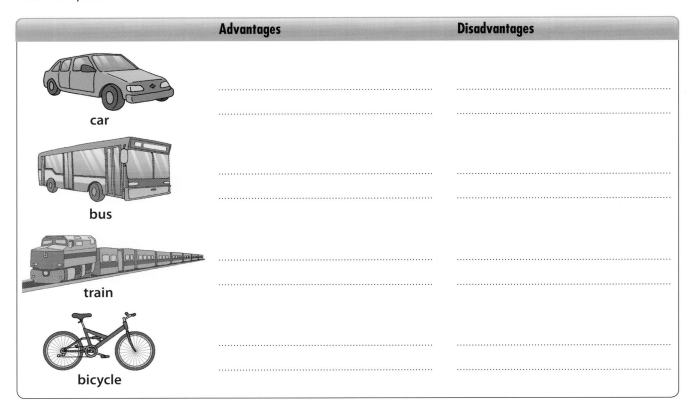

	Advantages	Disadvantages
car		
bus		
train		
bicycle		

B Convince another pair to leave their cars at home. Give as many reasons as you can why another form of transportation is better.

"If you drive a car every day, you're going to spend a lot of money on gas."

8 WHAT DID THEY SAY?

Watch the video and complete the conversation. Then practice it.

Jessica and Will warn Luis about the expenses of owning a car.

Jessica: People ....*used*.... ....*to*........ pay for things with cash. They
didn't buy on credit. ....
money to buy the car, you're ....
.... that debt for years.

Will: And even .... you .... the debt,
you're going to have to spend a lot of .... on the car.
You're going to .... to pay for ....
insurance, and you're going to .... to pay for
....

Jessica: Yeah, and you're going to have to pay for ....
And, if you're not .... , you're going to pay
parking .... It all ....

Luis: You're right. I didn't think .... the expenses.

Jessica: After graduation, I'm still going to ....
.... to work. But that's OK with me. Public transportation
in .... city is .... efficient.

9 TALKING ABOUT THE PAST, PRESENT, AND FUTURE

A Complete each sentence with at least two of the phrases
in the box. Then compare with a partner.

In the past, people used to . . .

1. ....

2. ....

Today, many people . . .

3. ....

4. ....

In the future, people will . . .

5. ....

6. ....

> think it's safer to get a job before
>   you buy a car
> pay for things with cash
> take the bus to work
> not buy things on credit
> establish credit through loans
> walk or bike to work more often

B Write two more sentences of your own about transportation in the
past, present, and future. Take turns reading them to a partner.

1. ....

2. ....

10 The job interview

1 CULTURE

Nearly 50 percent of North American college students have an internship at some point during college. In Canada, internships are called *co-ops*. A co-op, or internship, is like a temporary job, usually related to the student's major. Internships often take place during the summer when students are not in school. Others may be part-time during the school year. Some colleges offer course credit for doing an internship, and some employers pay interns a small wage. All internships allow students to gain experience in a new field. Interning is a great way to break into a company because employers often hire the former interns after they graduate.

Have you ever had a part-time job or internship? What did you do? Where would you like to work?

2 VOCABULARY *Getting a job*

PAIR WORK What questions would a job interviewer ask at a fast-food restaurant? Match the parts of the sentences. Then add two questions of your own.

1. Where did you — want to work here?
2. What are your — find out about this job?
3. Why do you — well with children?
4. Do you like — qualifications?
5. Do you get along — good with money?
6. Are you — working with people?

7. ....

8. ....

3 GUESS THE STORY

PAIR WORK What do you think each job candidate is like? Write a few words for each person.

Susan	Scott
professional	....
....	....

Susan

Scott

4 *GET THE PICTURE*

Complete the sentences. Then compare with a partner.

1. Mario Verdi is the ....
2. Danielle Derby is the ....
3. Susan and Scott are applying for an ....
4. Susan is quite skilled with ....
5. Scott enjoys working with ....
6. Mario likes .... Danielle prefers ....

5 *WHO SAID WHAT?*

A Who said the sentences below? Check (✓) the correct answers. Then compare with a partner.

	Danielle	Susan	Scott	Mario
1. I know all of the main design programs.	☐	✓	☐	☐
2. Would you be able to create a banner ad for a web page?	☐	☐	☐	☐
3. I love sports, and I love marketing.	☐	☐	☐	☐
4. I see you're quite skilled with computers.	☐	☐	☐	☐
5. Do you have any sales experience?	☐	☐	☐	☐
6. I can sell anything.	☐	☐	☐	☐
7. I love being busy.	☐	☐	☐	☐
8. I don't mind trying new things because I'm a very fast learner.	☐	☐	☐	☐

WHAT'S YOUR OPINION?

A What skills does the internship require? Write two more skills in the chart.

Job skills	Susan	Scott
Design skills	☐	☐
Computer skills	☐	☐
Other:	☐	☐
Other:	☐	☐

B Does Susan have the skills? Does Scott have the skills? Check (✓) the correct answers.

C (PAIR WORK) Discuss who you think is best for the job and why.

A: I think Scott has more of the skills the job needs. He said he's good with numbers.
B: Oh, I don't think so. I think when he says he's good at computers, he's exaggerating.

☰ Follow-up

7 INTERVIEW

(PAIR WORK) Interview a classmate for an internship. Use the questions in Exercise 2 and in the video to help you. Start like this:

A: Why do you want an internship here?
B: Well, I'm very creative. . . .

8 JOB SKILLS

A (PAIR WORK) What do a salesperson and a graphic designer need to be good at? Choose from these phrases and add other ideas of your own.

managing money
solving problems
using computers

using their visual sense
getting along with people

B (GROUP WORK) Now play a game. What skills do people with these jobs need? Take turns giving your ideas. Think of as many things as you can. The person with the most ideas wins.

a chef   a firefighter   a teacher

C What are you good at? Tell your group. Your classmates will suggest an appropriate career for you!

A manager needs to be good at managing money.

☰ Language close-up

9 WHAT DID THEY SAY?

Watch the video and complete the conversation. Then practice it.

Danielle and Mario interview an internship candidate.

Mario: You have a very ......impressive...... résumé, Susan. .... us about ....

Susan: Well, Mr. Verdi, I'm .... and I .... that my artistic ....

would .... well here.

Danielle: I see you're quite .... with ....

Susan: Yes. I .... all the .... design .... And I'm actually

.... a .... for my father's ...., and I'm ....

a 3-D software .... this ....

Danielle: Excellent! But won't you be ....

for an internship?

Susan: Oh, no. I .... busy.

10 SHORT RESPONSES *Giving personal information*

A Write personal responses to these statements, choosing from
the expressions below. Then compare with a partner.

So am I.	Neither am I.	I am.	I'm not.
So do I.	Neither do I.	I do.	I don't.
So can I.	Neither can I.	I can.	I can't.

1. I like working with numbers. ....

2. I enjoy working with computers. ....

3. I'm not good at managing money. ....

4. I don't like doing office work. ....

5. I can sell anything. ....

6. I can't type very fast. ....

B Now write four new statements about yourself and read them to your
partner. Your partner will respond with one of the expressions above.

1. ....

2. ....

3. ....

4. ....

Two brothers in Peru

1 CULTURE

Peru is located in western South America. It is bordered by the Pacific coast, divided by the Andes Mountains, and is partly covered by the Amazon Rain Forest. Nearly 30 million people live in this diverse land. Spanish is the official language, but many people speak the native language, Quechua. Peru is the home of Machu Picchu, an archaeological site that once was a busy Incan city. It was abandoned about 500 years ago but is now a popular destination for tourists, historians, and hikers. Machu Picchu is a UNESCO World Heritage site and an important cultural attraction.

Would you like to visit Machu Picchu? Why or why not?
What do you enjoy most about traveling?

2 VOCABULARY Sightseeing

A **PAIR WORK** What can you do when you travel to a historic site? Put the words in the chart. Can you add two more words?

✓ancient ruins	go hiking	join a tour group	temples
eat at restaurants	hot springs	shop at local markets	

Things to see	Things to do
ancient ruins	

B Which things in your chart do you like to do the most?

3 GUESS THE FACTS

Watch the first 30 seconds of the video with the sound off.
Answer these questions.

Who are the people in the video?
What do you think the video is going to show?

GET THE PICTURE

A These are the things that Derek and Paul did in Peru. Put the pictures in order (1 to 5).

B Now write the correct sentence under each picture. Compare with a partner.

They climbed Huayna Picchu for a different view.　　　They took the train back to Cusco.
They saw the Incas' "riding lawnmower," the llama.　✓ They hiked the Inca Trail to Machu Picchu.
They ate fruits and vegetables from local markets.

....　..　They hiked the Inca Trail to

....　..　Machu Picchu.

....　..

....　..

5 **WHAT'S YOUR OPINION?**

A What do you think of Derek and Paul's trip? Rate each part of the
trip from 1 (very interesting) to 5 (not interesting). Circle the numbers.

1. Exploring Machu Picchu	1	2	3	4	5
2. Visiting the town of Aguas Calientes	1	2	3	4	5
3. Seeing the open market with fruits and vegetables	1	2	3	4	5
4. Learning about the history of Machu Picchu	1	2	3	4	5
5. Climbing Huayna Picchu	1	2	3	4	5

B **PAIR WORK** Compare opinions.

A: What did you think of exploring Machu Picchu?　　B: It looked fun. I gave it a 1. How about you? . . .

6 WATCH FOR DETAILS

Write one thing that you learned about the people, places, or things below. Then compare with a partner.

1. Machu Picchu ....

2. The Inca ....

3. Aguas Calientes ....

4. Huayna Picchu ....

5. Paul and Derek ....

☰ Follow-up

7 A DAY AT MACHU PICCHU

A **GROUP WORK** Use your knowledge of Machu Picchu to plan three things to do. Choose from the suggestions in the tourist brochure below.

Machu Picchu

Bus or hike to Machu Picchu.

Join a tour of Machu Picchu.

Learn about the history of Hiram Bingham and the site.

See llamas.

Hike to Huayna Picchu.

Explore and shop in the local markets.

Start like this:

A: I'd like to learn about Hiram Bingham.
B: So would I. I wonder what year he was born. . . .

B **CLASS ACTIVITY** Compare answers as a class.

8 WHAT DID HE SAY?

Watch the video and complete the description. Then compare with a partner.

Paul talks about the construction of Machu Picchu.

Machu Picchu, which means "Old Peak," ....was.... ....constructed.... around 1450. .... , as the empire collapsed .... the Spanish, it .... abandoned, roughly 100 years .... Machu Picchu .... the outside ....

In 1911, the site .... explorer and historian Hiram Bingham .... the .... of some .... residents. He .... the .... job of clearing .... hundreds of .... of .... growth from the ....

9 THE PASSIVE Giving factual information

A Imagine that Paul and Derek said these things about Machu Picchu. Complete the sentences using the verbs in parentheses. Then compare with a partner.

1. The historic site of Machu Picchu ....is located......... in Peru. (locate)
2. Tourists .... all the comforts of home in Aguas Calientes. (offer)
3. This entire hotel .... out by tourists. (rent)
4. Ancient techniques .... still .... by craftsmen in this town. (use)
5. The buildings .... out of blocks of stone. (build)
6. The site .... by half a million people a year! (visit)

B Now write five sentences about your own city using the passive. Compare around the class.

1. ....
2. ....
3. ....
4. ....
5. ....

12 Profile: A TV reporter

1 CULTURE

Changes in technology have changed journalism. News media have shifted from the printed word of newspapers and magazines to the Internet. Reporters still report on current events, but on the Internet, stories often include photos, videos, and frequent updates throughout the day. Today, a reporter can carry his or her own video camera or even report using a cell phone. And as more readers are posting their own news stories and opinions online, the face of journalism is changing.

Where do you get your news?
What do you think is the biggest change to journalism today?
How do you think journalism will change in the next 10 years?

2 VOCABULARY *The life of a reporter*

PAIR WORK Put the words in the word map.

✓ car accident	house fire	learning a language	radio reporter	TV reporter
corruption	laptop computer	organized crime	riding a bike	video camera

Types of reporters
....
....

Technology to produce stories
....
....

The Life of a Reporter

Story assignments
car accident
....
....
....

Hobbies
....
....

3 GUESS THE FACTS

Watch the first minute and a half of the video with the sound off.
Answer these questions.

1. Where do you think this person works?

   ....

2. Where do you think he lives?

   ....

3. What hobbies do you think he has?

   ....

Watch the video

4 GET THE PICTURE

Look at your answers to Exercise 3. Did you guess correctly? Correct your
answers. Then compare with a partner.

5 WATCH FOR DETAILS

Check (✓) **True** or **False**. Then correct the false statements. Compare with a partner.

	True	False	
1. Kai Nagata owns the Canadian Broadcasting Company (CBC).	☐	✓	Kai works for the CBC.
2. The CBC news network is in Canada.	☐	☐	....
3. When Kai first moved to Montreal, he spoke French very well.	☐	☐	....
4. Kai started out as a TV reporter.	☐	☐	....
5. Kai tells his stories in words.	☐	☐	....
6. Kai uses a laptop computer to produce stories.	☐	☐	....
7. Kai wants to tell stories about other countries.	☐	☐	....
8. Lately, Kai has been assigned to stories about corruption.	☐	☐	....
9. Kai likes knowing what stories he'll be assigned.	☐	☐	....
10. Kai thinks he will be a journalist for a short time.	☐	☐	....

6 WHAT'S YOUR OPINION?

A (PAIR WORK) What stories has Kai Nagata covered? Check (✓) your answers. Can you add one or two more stories that you heard mentioned? Then compare with a partner.

☐ corruption

☐ demonstration

☐ house fire

☐ ....

☐ inflation

☐ ....

B If you were a reporter, which stories in part A would you like to cover? Which wouldn't you like to cover? Think of two more stories you would like to cover. Write them below. Discuss with a partner.

1. ....   2. ....

☰ Follow-up

7 ROLE PLAY *How long have you been . . . ?*

A (PAIR WORK) Imagine that you are a reporter interviewing your partner for a profile story. Ask questions about past and current interests. Then switch places. Start like this:

A: What things did you like when you were a kid?
B: When I was little, I liked . . .
A: What are you interested in now?
B: Well, lately I've been . . .

B (GROUP WORK) Take turns telling your group about what your partner has been doing. Try to use some of the phrases in the box below.

began as	has been able to	moved to
first started	has been thinking about	plans to
had	has been working on	wanted to

8 WHAT DID HE SAY?

Watch the video and complete the commentary. Then compare with a partner.

Kai Nagata talks about his career as a reporter.

When I first ......started...... off at the CBC, I

.... on the radio side. I went out as a radio

reporter, and I .... all the same news stories

as the TV reporters, but only for audio. Then I ....

.... and moved over to television, and so, for the

last year, I've .... all my stories visually.

In the .... , TV reporters ....

.... rely on a big crew, a big team .... lots of .... ,

complicated equipment. But with .... technology, I ....

.... a whole TV story on my own. I've .... stories for

TV .... just a video camera in my backpack .... a laptop

computer.

9 VERB TENSES *Talking about the past and present*

A Match phrases from A and B and write four sentences. Then compare with a partner.

A

Kai has been learning French
Kai was promoted to the TV side
Kai has been riding his bike
Kai's ancestors immigrated to Canada
Kai reported simple stories

B

since he was a kid.
since he arrived in Montreal.
after working as a radio reporter.
when he first joined the CBC.
more than a hundred years ago.

1. Kai has been learning French since he arrived in Montreal.

2. ....

3. ....

4. ....

5. ....

B Now complete these sentences with information about yourself.
Compare with a partner.

1. I was .... when I ....

2. While I was .... , I became interested in ....

3. I've been .... for the last ....

Street performers

☰ Preview

1 CULTURE

Visitors to Boston, Massachusetts should not miss Faneuil (*fan-yule*) Hall Marketplace. It is one of the United States' top tourist sites. This historic marketplace opened in 1742 and was a market and the site of famous meetings. It is near the water, and there are many restaurants and shops for people to enjoy. What makes the marketplace really exciting, though, is the free entertainment. Every day the marketplace fills with street performers and the people who come to watch them.

Faneuil Hall Marketplace

Are street performers popular in your country?
Would you stop to watch a street performer?
Do you think people should give money to street performers?
   Why or why not?

2 VOCABULARY *Street performers*

A **PAIR WORK** Write the correct word(s) under each picture.

> ✓an acrobat   an accordion player   a balloon man   a clown   a dance troupe   a magician

1. ....

2. an acrobat

3. ....

4. ....

5. ....

6. ....

B Can you think of four more types of street performers? Write them below.

1. ....   2. ....   3. ....   4. ....

GUESS THE FACTS

Watch the first minute of the video with the sound off. Who is the host?

a reporter   a tour guide   a tourist

Watch the video

 GET THE PICTURE

Write the type of performer under each picture. Which performers did the host talk
to or talk about? Check (✓) the correct answers. Then compare with a partner.

....

....

 WATCH FOR DETAILS

What are these people's opinions of the performers? Write at least two words.
Then compare with a partner.

....
....
....

6 WHAT'S YOUR OPINION?

A What do you think of the performers? Rate each performance from 1 (very good) to 5 (poor). Circle the numbers.

1	1	1	1
2	2	2	2
3	3	3	3
4	4	4	4
5	5	5	5

B **PAIR WORK** Compare opinions. Choose words from the box or use words of your own.

amazing	energetic	great	surprised
amusing	entertaining	interesting	talented
boring	excellent	fascinating	unbelievable
creative	fun	silly	

A: What did you think of the balloon man?
B: I thought he was creative. I gave him a 2. How about you? . . .

☰ Follow-up

7 HIRE A PERFORMER

GROUP WORK Imagine you are planning a party and want to hire a performer or group of performers. Which of these performers would you like to hire? Why?

A: I think it would be great to hire a magician.
B: Why?
A: Well, because magicians are entertaining. . . .

a mime   **a guitarist**   **a magician**   **a pianist**   **a rock band**

8 WHAT DID THEY SAY?

Watch the video and complete the interview. Then compare with a partner.

The host asks a woman what she thought of a street performer.

Host: So what did you ....think...... about his .... ?

Woman: I .... by what he could do, and all the things he .... make

out of balloons! This man is .... It .... you feel like you're a

.... again. I think .... both really ....

what he's doing. It's .... to .... by someone on the street, and

.... , they're just making something .... out of a ....

9 PARTICIPLES Giving opinions

A Rewrite these sentences using present and past participles.
Then compare with a partner.

1. The balloon man entertained me.

   The balloon man was entertaining.

   I was entertained by the balloon man.

2. The musician surprised me.

   ....

   ....

3. The dance troupe energized me.

   ....

   ....

4. The host amused me.

   ....

   ....

B Now change your sentences to give your true opinions. Read them to a partner.

C Complete the chart. Then compare with a partner.

Something you find entertaining	Something you find boring
I find .... entertaining.	....

Something you find amusing	Something you find surprising
....	....

14 The body language of business

☰ Preview

1 CULTURE

Picture yourself riding in an elevator alone. What happens when someone else enters the elevator? Where do you both stand? Do you make eye contact? Where do people stand when there are four people? Imagine that you enter a crowded elevator, face everyone, make eye contact, and smile. What would people do? What would they think about you? There are unspoken rules for riding in an elevator, just as there are cultural rules for how close we stand to people, the gestures we use, and how much eye contact is polite. But there is one gesture that is universally understood: a smile.

*In your country, what gesture do you use when you meet someone
for the first time? How do you greet an old friend?
What gestures are considered rude?*

2 VOCABULARY *Body language*

PAIR WORK Which word do you think best describes the people below?
Check (✓) the correct word.

1. ✔ friendly
   ☐ nervous

2. ☐ bored
   ☐ interested

3. ☐ confident
   ☐ lazy

4. ☐ approachable
   ☐ surprised

5. ☐ confused
   ☐ sincere

3 GUESS THE FACTS

Watch the first 30 seconds of the video with the sound off.
What is your first impression of the woman in the job interview?
Write down a few words that describe her body language.

....

Watch the video

4 GET THE PICTURE

Check (✓) the correct answers. Then compare with a partner.

1. The host says you can make a good
   first impression with . . .
   ☐ what you say.
   ☐ your body language.

2. The host says you have seven seconds
   to show . . .
   ☐ your credibility, confidence, and competence.
   ☐ your job skills and professional experience.

5 WATCH FOR DETAILS

Write the correct sentence under each picture. Then compare with a partner.

> ✓ Adjust your attitude.   Make eye contact.   Shake hands.   Stand tall.
> Lean in slightly.   Raise your eyebrows.   Smile.

1. ....

2. ....

3. ....

4. ....

5. ....

6. ....

7. Adjust your attitude.

6 WHAT DOES IT MEAN?

What gestures can you use to convey these attitudes? Check (✓) all the correct answers.
Then compare with a partner.

	smile	raise eyebrows	lean in slightly	make eye contact
1. interested	☐	☐	☐	☐
2. friendly	☐	☐	☐	☐
3. open	☐	☐	☐	☐
4. acknowledging	☐	☐	☐	☐
5. approachable	☐	☐	☐	☐
6. engaged	☐	☐	☐	☐

☰ Follow-up

7 GESTURES

A PAIR WORK What are some other gestures you might make during
a job interview? Add two gestures to the list. Then compare with a partner.

1. Adjust your attitude.
2. Stand tall.
3. Smile.
4. Make eye contact.
5. Raise your eyebrows.
6. Lean in slightly.
7. Shake hands.
8. ....
9. ....

B Act out each gesture from part A and have your partner
guess which one it is.

8 ROLE PLAY

PAIR WORK Practice making good first impressions.
Take turns acting as the interviewer and interviewee.
Remember to use gestures from the video. Start like this:

A: Hello, I'm (name). (shakes hands)
B: I'm (name). Thank you for coming in. (smiles)

☰ Language close-up

9 WHAT DID SHE SAY?

Watch the video and complete the descriptions. Then compare with a partner.

The host explains some ways to make a positive first impression.

First, adjust your attitude. ......Don't...... ......wait...... until you ....
the interview room to .... Before you ....
through the door, ... about the situation and ....
a conscious choice about the .... you want to embody.
.... that attract .... include .... ,
.... , approachable, and ....

*   *   *

Make eye contact. .... at someone's .... transmits
energy and indicates .... and ....
.... the interviewer's eyes .... enough to notice
what .... they are. With this one ....
technique, ... dramatically increase ....
likeability factor.

10 MODALS AND ADVERBS *Expressing probability*

A Complete each conversation with a logical answer. Then compare with a partner.

1. A: I just had a job interview. The interviewer didn't offer to shake my hand.
   B: Maybe it means ....

2. A: I sent my friend three text messages, but she didn't respond.
   B: It could mean ....

3. A: My boss was late for our meeting. And she didn't make eye contact at first.
   B: It may mean ....

4. A: I just got this new coat, and I really like it. But sometimes I see people
      whispering.
   B: Perhaps it means ....

B **PAIR WORK** Now have similar conversations about
real or imaginary situations in your own life.

A: My friend Steve doesn't answer my text messages.
B: Maybe it means . . .

Sticky situations

1 CULTURE

In a recent survey, people in the United States were asked to describe their most embarrassing moments during a visit to someone's home. Here are the top answers:

- Dressing incorrectly for the occasion.
- Arriving on the wrong day or wrong time.
- Spilling something or breaking something valuable.
- Saying something by mistake that offended the host.
- Forgetting someone's name.

Would the same things be embarrassing in your culture? Why or why not?
What was your most embarrassing moment during a visit to someone's home?

Almost everyone has dressed the wrong way at least once!

2 VOCABULARY *Problems with guests*

PAIR WORK Do you know these nouns and verbs? Complete the chart. (If you don't know a word, look it up in your dictionary.) Then take turns answering the questions below.

Verb	Noun	Verb	Noun
apologize	_apology_	misunderstand	....
....	approval	....	offer
invite	....	....	realization
....	lie	....	reminder

1. Have you apologized for anything recently?
2. What's something a person might lie about?
3. Have you had a problem because someone misunderstood you recently?
4. Has someone offered you something nice recently?
5. Have you had to remind someone to do something lately?

3 GUESS THE FACTS

Watch the video with the sound off. What three embarrassing situations do you see?

Watch the video

4 GET THE PICTURE

A What happened to these people? Write the correct sentence under each picture.

This person didn't like what the host served for dinner.
This person arrived too early for a party.
A dinner guest stayed too late at this person's house.
This person served food her guest didn't like.

A dinner guest stayed too late at this person's house.

Her husband fell asleep at the table.

B Now write one more piece of information under each picture. Compare with a partner.

C **PAIR WORK** Take turns. Describe what happened to each person.

"This woman invited her boss over for dinner. They had a good time, but her boss wouldn't leave. Her husband fell asleep. . . ."

5 WATCH FOR DETAILS

A What are these people's opinions about the situations? Write the correct number in each box. Then compare with a partner.

Situation 1

The guest should have . . .   The host should have . . .

1. apologized and offered to help.   1. asked the guest to run an errand.
2. pretended to have an errand to run.   2. put the guest to work.
3. left quickly and come back later.

Situation 2

The host should have . . .

1. lied and said she had to get up early.
2. pretended she wasn't tired.
3. reminded her boss it was late.
4. asked her boss to do the dishes.

Situation 3

The guest should have . . .   The host should have . . .

1. gone home before eating.   1. asked her guests if they had food allergies.
2. lied and said she was allergic to seafood.   2. asked her guests to bring food.
3. eaten it anyway.   3. eaten it anyway.

B **PAIR WORK** Which people do you agree with? Take turns sharing your opinions.

A: I agree with her *(points to photo)*. The guest should have . . .
B: I think his suggestion is better *(points)*. The guest should have . . .

Follow-up

6 WHAT WOULD YOU HAVE DONE?

GROUP WORK Take turns describing awkward or embarrassing situations you've been in. Say what you did. Your classmates will tell you what they would have done.

A: I realized I forgot my best friend's birthday, so I gave her some flowers two weeks later and apologized. What would you have done?

B: Well, I think I would have . . .

Language close-up

7 WHAT DID THEY SAY?

People are describing difficult situations involving guests.

A Watch the first situation. Complete the guest's description.

I was ......*invited*...... to a .... , and I .... an hour

.... I thought it would .... me .... to get

there. Well, Rebecca .... to the door .... sweatpants

and an old T-shirt. . . . I could .... the shower .... in the

background, and of course, ... a single guest was ....

B Now watch the second situation. Complete the host's description.

I .... my boss and her husband to .... the other

.... We had a .... time, but she just wouldn't

.... By .... , my .... and I were so

.... Finally, my husband fell .... at the table. My boss

was very .... when she .... it was so ....

I just .... know what to do when a guest won't go ....

8 WOULD HAVE *AND* SHOULD HAVE *Giving suggestions*

A **PAIR WORK** Can you think of suggestions for these situations? Write statements using **would have** and **should have**. Then compare around the class. Who has the best suggestions?

1. A guest arrived on the wrong day for the party.

   The guest *should have apologized and gone home* .

   If I were the host, I *would have . . .* .

2. A dinner guest broke a valuable dish.

   If I were the guest, I ....

   The host ....

3. Two dinner guests got into a big argument.

   The guests ....

   If I were the host, I ....

4. The host discovered she didn't have enough food.

   The guests ....

   If I were the host, I ....

It's my birthday!

☰ Preview

1 CULTURE

In the United States and Canada, birthdays are celebrated at all ages and in different ways. There is no typical party; some are large and others are small. For children, parents throw parties at home or at a child-themed restaurant. Guests are expected to bring presents. For adults, parties are held at home or at a restaurant or club. Presents aren't usually expected, but for parties at home, it's always good to bring some food or drink for the host. Two things you can expect at all birthday parties: a cake with candles and people singing "Happy Birthday to You."

How do people in your country celebrate birthdays?
Are certain birthdays more important to celebrate than others?
What are guests expected to do for a birthday?

2 VOCABULARY *Adjectives*

PAIR WORK How would you feel in the situations below? Choose adjectives from the box.

amused	delighted	enthusiastic	nervous	shy
angry	disappointed	excited	pleased	upset
bored	embarrassed	interested	relaxed	worried

1. You are a dinner guest at someone's house. Your host offers you food you don't like.

   A: I think I'd feel worried. How can I avoid eating it and not offend my host?

   B: Really? I'd be relaxed. Just eat a little bit and say you had a big lunch.

2. Your best friend gives you a gift that you really don't like.

3. Someone forgets an appointment with you.

4. You meet someone you like at a party. The next day you run into the person at the supermarket.

5. Someone talks to you at the store. You realize it's someone you've met before, but you can't remember the person's name.

3 GUESS THE STORY

Watch the first two minutes of the video with the sound off.
What do you think Tim is doing? Check (✓) your answer.

- ☐ trying to make plans
- ☐ trying to get out of plans
- ☐ trying to find someone

Watch the video

4 GET THE PICTURE

How do you think these people really felt? Check (✓) the best answers.
Then compare with a partner.

1. How did Sofia act when she told Tim everyone was busy?
   - ☐ angry
   - ☐ sympathetic

2. How did Tim feel when Steve said he was busy Saturday?
   - ☐ disappointed
   - ☐ pleased

3. Was Sofia pleased with Steve's text message?
   - ☐ definitely
   - ☐ probably not

4. How did Tim feel when he arrived at Sofia's house?
   - ☐ happy to see her, but disappointed that no one else could come
   - ☐ confused that Sofia was the only person there

5. What was Tim's reaction when Sofia turned on the video?
   - ☐ He was angry that his friends surprised him.
   - ☐ He was delighted that his friends surprised him.

5 MAKING INFERENCES

Who said what? Check (✓) the person who said each sentence.
Was the person lying, or being sincere? On the line,
write **L** for lying or **S** for sincere. Compare with a partner.

1. Everyone told me they were busy. □ .... ✓ ...L.. □ .... □ ....

2. I didn't know you were into salsa dancing. □ .... □ .... □ .... □ ....

3. We're on a conference call. □ .... □ .... □ .... □ ....

4. John can't come to your dinner Saturday. □ .... □ .... □ .... □ ....

5. Maybe you guys can stop by the club afterwards. □ .... □ .... □ .... □ ....

6. I guess you'll miss my birthday. Too bad. □ .... □ .... □ .... □ ....

☰ Follow-up

6 POLITE RESPONSES

A PAIR WORK Imagine you're talking with friends. Complete the
conversations below with polite responses or excuses. Then act them out.

1. A: Why don't we play chess? It's one of my favorite games!
   B: It's one of my favorite games, too. ....

2. A: Do you want to go see the new science fiction movie on Saturday?
   B: ....

3. A: We're having something special for dinner. I hope you like spicy food!
   B: ....

4. A: What do you think of this poem I wrote?
   B: ....

B Now act out at least two new conversations of your own.
You can make them long or short. Make sure not to hurt your
partner's feelings!

Language close-up

7 WHAT DID THEY SAY?

Watch the video and complete the conversation. Then practice it.

Jessica and John make excuses not to come to Tim's birthday party.

Jessica: John can't come to ....your.... ....dinner.... Saturday.
I just asked him. And ....
that he has other plans.

John: I did?

Jessica: Yeah, you .... that you were playing
guitar with your .... , uh, someplace. In fact, I was very ....
that you .... playing. Very *surprised*.

John: Oh, yeah. .... , I'm busy . . . playing . . . on Saturday. ....

Tim: .... you weren't in the band anymore.

John: This is my farewell concert. I .... do it.

Tim: I guess you'll miss my birthday. ....

John: Yeah, but I can't .... You know .... it is. Maybe
.... can stop by the club ....

Tim: Sure. Yeah. Thanks. That sounds ....

8 REPORTED SPEECH *He said, she said*

A Report what each person said. Then compare with a partner.

1. "Maybe they can change their plans." (Tim)
   Tim said maybe they could change their plans.

2. "I'm salsa dancing." (Steve)
   ....

3. "I'll make it up to you." (Steve to Tim)
   ....

4. "We're on a conference call." (Jessica)
   ....

5. "John can't come to dinner." (Jessica)
   ....

"I'm salsa dancing."

B **CLASS ACTIVITY** Ask several classmates what they think of
the things in the box. Write down their answers. Then report
their opinions to the class.

A: What do you think of wrestling?
B: I think it's awful.
A: Tina said she thought wrestling was awful. . . .

> jazz music
> motorcycles
> old movies
> pet costumes
> vegetarian food
> wrestling

interchange

FOURTH EDITION

Jack C. Richards
With Jonathan Hull and Susan Proctor

Series Editor: David Bohlke

CAMBRIDGE
UNIVERSITY PRESS

WORKBOOK 2B

Contents

Credits

Illustrations

Andrezzinho: 11; **Daniel Baxter:** 28, 38, 41, 48, 88; **Carlos Diaz:** 6, 77, 94; **Jada Fitch:** 17, 42; **Tim Foley:** 22, 80; **Dylan Gibson:** 86, 92; **Chuck Gonzales:** 4, 34, 67; **Joaquin Gonzalez:** 35, 59; **Dan Hubig:** 90; **Trevor Keen:** 13, 21 (*bottom*), 55, 72, 83 (*top*); **KJA-artists:** 2, 36, 50 (*left and center*), 84, 91; **Greg Lawhun:** 16, 68, 87

Monika Melnychuk: 39 (*right*) **Karen Minot:** 10, 15, 27, 65, 89; **Ortelius Design:** 30 (*map*), 64; **Rob Schuster:** 30, 45, 51, 54, 63, 73, 83 (*bottom center*), 93; **Daniel Vasconcellos:** 19, 31, 71; **James Yamasaki:** 1, 32, 79, 85; **Rose Zgodzinski:** 18, 39 (*left*), 40, 57, 75, 78, 81; **Carol Zuber-Mallison:** 3, 9, 21(*top*), 33, 50 (*top and bottom*), 69, 87

Photos

3 © Allstar Picture Library/Alamy

5 © Denkou Images/Alamy

7 (*top, left to right*) © Glowimages/Getty Images; © Dennis MacDonald/age footstock; (*middle, left to right*) © Stacy Walsh Rosenstock/Alamy; © Bill Freeman/Alamy; (*bottom, left to right*) © Lee Snider/The Image Works; © Richard Lord/PhotoEdit

8 © Michael Dwyer/Alamy

10 (*top, left to right*) © Jane Sweeney/Robert Harding World Imagery/Corbis; © Jon Arnold Images Ltd/Alamy; © VisualHongKong/Alamy; © One-image photography/Alamy

12 © Jason O. Watson/Alamy

14 (*right, top to bottom*) © Exactostock/SuperStock; © Frank van den Bergh/iStockphoto

18 (*top right*) © Alberto Pomares/iStockphoto; (*bottom, left to right*) © Betty Johnson/Dbimages/Alamy; © Mustafa Ozer/AFP/Getty Images

20 © iStockphoto/Thinkstock

23 © Tupporn Sirichoo/iStockphoto

25 © RubberBall/SuperStock

27 (*left, top to bottom*) © Licia Rubinstein/iStockphoto; © Raga Jose Fuste/Prisma Bildagentur AG/Alamy; © Radharcimages.com/Alamy

29 © Yagi Studio/Digital Vision/Getty Images

30 (*top inset*) © iStockphoto/Thinkstock; (*middle*) © Andrey Devyatov/iStockphoto

37 (*left to right*) © i love images/Alamy; © Ricardoazoury/iStockphoto; © Erik Simonsen/Photographer's Choice/Getty Images; © Angelo Arcadi/iStockphoto; © Martyn Goddard/Corbis

43 (*right, top to bottom*) © Daniel Dempster Photography/Alamy; © Tetra Images/Getty Images

46 (*right, top to bottom*) © Glow Asia/Alamy; © David Young-Wolff/PhotoEdit

47 (*left to right*) © Eye Ubiquitous/SuperStock; © Hisham Ibrahim/Photographer's Choice/Getty Images; © Bill Bachmann/Alamy; © Brand X Pictures/Thinkstock

49 © Bettmann/Corbis

52 © Hermann Erber/LOOK Die Bildagentur der Fotografen GmbH/Alamy

54 © Bruno Perousse/age footstock

58 (*top left*) © Vadym Drobot/Shutterstock; (*middle right*) © Juan Carlos Tinjaca/Shutterstock; (*middle left*) © Alena Ozerova/Shutterstock; (*bottom right*) © Stuart Jenner/Shutterstock; (*bottom left*) © iStockphoto/Thinkstock

61 © Florian Kopp/Imagebroker/Alamy

62 (*top, left to right*) © Luciano Mortula/Shutterstock; © Anibal Trejo/Shutterstock; © Julian Love/John Warburton-Lee Photography/Alamy; (*middle, left to right*) © Bill Bachman/Alamy; © Juergen Richter/LOOK Die Bildagentur der Fotografen GmbH/Alamy; © Goran Bogicevic/Shutterstock

63 (*middle, top to bottom*) © Bernardo Galmarini/Alamy; © Ariadne Van Zandbergen/Alamy

64 © Josef Polleross/The Image Works

65 (*top right*) © Robert Landau/Surf/Corbis; (*bottom right*) © Travel Pictures/Alamy

66 © Hulton-Deutsch Collection/Historical/Corbis

69 © Globe Photos/ZUMAPRESS/NEWSCOM

70 © Han Myung-Gu/WireImage/Getty Images

73 © WALT DISNEY PICTURES/Album/NEWSCOM

74 © XPhantom/Shutterstock

75 (*top left*) © Bettmann/Corbis; (*top right*) © Sunset Boulevard/Historical/Corbis

76 © Buyenlarge/Archive Photos/Getty Images

78 © LIONSGATE/Album/NEWSCOM

82 © Mark Gibson/Danita Delimont Photography/NEWSCOM

83 (*all*) © ahmet urkac/Shutterstock

95 © Workbook Stock/Getty Images

96 © maXx images/SuperStock

Times have changed!

1 **Complete this passage with the verbs in the box. Use the past, present, or future tense.**

☐ buy	☐ drive	☐ have	☐ leave	☐ sell
☐ change	☑ go	☐ have to	☐ sell	☐ use

In many countries nowadays, food shopping takes very little time.
In the past, people _____*used to go*_____ to a different shop
for each type of item. For example, you _____ meat
at a butcher's shop and fish at a fish market. A fruit market
_____ fruits and vegetables. For dry goods, like
rice or beans, you _____ go to grocery stores.
Today, the supermarket or superstore _____ all these things. Once every week
or two, people _____ in their cars to these huge stores to buy everything – not
only food but also clothes, electronic goods, furniture, and medicine. But in the future, the way
we shop _____ again. Nowadays, many people _____
a computer at home. Soon, maybe, no one _____ home to go shopping.
Everyone _____ their computers to order everything online.

2 **Choose the correct responses.**

1. A: When did people travel by horse and carriage?

   B: _____

   • In the next few years.   • About 100 years ago.   • These days.

2. A: When might doctors find a cure for the flu?

   B: _____

   • Nowadays.   • In the next 50 years.   • A few years ago.

3. A: When did the first man go to the moon?

   B: _____

   • Sometime in the future.   • Today.   • More than 40 years ago.

4. A: When is everyone going to have a computer at home?

   B: _____

   • In the past.   • Right now.   • Soon.

3 Complete the sentences. Use the words given and ideas from the pictures.

1. These days, _people go to the_ _beach on vacation._ (beach)
   In the future, _they might go_ _to Mars on vacation._ (Mars)

2. In the past, _____
   _____ (collect records)
   Nowadays, _____
   _____ (download music)

3. A few years ago, _____
   _____ (desktops)
   Today, _____
   _____ (tablets)

4. A century or more ago, _____
   _____ (long dresses)
   These days, _____
   _____ (short skirts)

5. Nowadays, _____
   _____ (20 floors)
   Sometime in the future, _____
   _____ (250 floors)

4 *New forms of energy*

A Scan the article. Why do we need new forms of energy? According to the article, which countries produce each new form of energy?

THE FUTURE OF ENERGY

Energy is very important in modern life. People use energy to run machines, heat or cool their homes, cook, provide light, and transport people and products. Most energy nowadays comes from fossil fuels – petroleum, coal, and natural gas. However, burning fossil fuels causes pollution. Scientists are working to find other kinds of energy for the future. What might these sources of energy be?

Energy from wind All over the world, people use the power of wind. It turns windmills and moves sailboats. It is a clean source of energy, and there is lots of it, particularly in countries such as the Netherlands and Denmark. Unfortunately, if the wind does not blow, there is no wind energy.

Energy from water When water moves from a high place to a lower place, it makes energy. This energy creates electricity without pollution through the use of dams and water turbines. Laos plans to build 55 dams and become the "battery" of southeast Asia. Dams, however, cost a lot of money to build, so water energy is expensive.

Energy from the earth There is heat in rocks under the earth. Scientists use this heat to make geothermal energy. In Iceland, 87 percent of the population enjoys central heating from this energy source – and it costs less than half the price of using oil for central heating. Moreover, geothermal energy does not pollute. The problem is location – it's only available in a few places in the world.

Energy from the sun Solar panels on the roofs of houses can turn energy from the sun into electricity. These panels can create enough energy to heat or cool an entire house. In fact, some scientists say that if we build solar panels in just 1 percent of the Sahara Desert, in countries such as Algeria and Libya, there will be enough electricity for the entire world. However, solar energy is expensive to export.

Energy from living organisms Living organisms, such as plants and algae, can produce energy that is called biofuel. By 2017, about 90 percent of cars in Brazil will have "flex-fuel" engines – they can run on gasoline or biofuels. Biofuels are renewable. For example, sugarcane (used to make ethanol) can be produced every year. But some people say we should use farmland to produce food, not biofuels.

B Read the article. What is one advantage and one disadvantage of each type of energy? Complete the chart.

	Advantage	Disadvantage
wind power		
water power		
geothermal power		
solar power		
biofuels		

5 Choose the correct responses.

1. A: What if I get in shape this summer?

   B: _____

   • You might be able to come rock climbing with me.
   • You won't be able to come rock climbing with me.

2. A: What will happen if I stop exercising?

   B: _____

   • Well, you won't gain weight.
   • Well, you might gain weight.

3. A: What if I get a better job?

   B: _____

   • You won't be able to buy new clothes.
   • You'll be able to buy some new clothes.

4. A: What will happen if I don't get a summer job?

   B: _____

   • You'll probably have enough money for your school expenses.
   • You probably won't have enough money for your school expenses.

6 Verb pairs

A Which words go with which verbs? Complete the chart.

☐ a cold	☐ money
☑ energetic	☐ relaxed
☐ exercising	☐ weight
☐ married	☐ working

feel	get	lose	quit
energetic	_____	_____	_____
_____	_____	_____	_____

B Write sentences with *if*. Use some of the words in part A.

1. If I feel energetic, I might go for a walk. _____

2. _____

3. _____

4. _____

5. _____

7 Complete these sentences with your own information. Add a comma where necessary.

> **Grammar note: Conditional sentences with if clauses**
>
> **The if clause can come before or after the main clause.**
> **Before the main clause, add a comma.**
> If I move to a cheaper apartment, I'll be able to buy a car.
> **After the main clause, do not add a comma.**
> I'll be able to buy a car if I move to a cheaper apartment.

1. If I go shopping on Saturday, _I might spend too much money._
2. I'll feel healthier _____
3. If I get more exercise _____
4. If I don't get good grades in school _____
5. I might get more sleep _____
6. I'll be happy _____

8 *Nouns and adjectives*

A Complete the chart with another form of the word given.

Noun	Adjective	Noun	Adjective
energy	_____	_____	medical
_____	environmental	success	_____
health	_____		

B Complete the sentences. Use words in part A.

1. There have been lots of _____medical_____ advances in the past half century, but there is still no cure for the common cold.

2. There are a lot of _____ problems in my country. There's too much air pollution, and the rivers are dirty.

3. My _____ is not as good as it used to be. So, I've decided to eat better food and go swimming every day.

4. My party was a great _____ . I think I might have another one soon!

5. If I start exercising more often, I might have more _____ .

9 **Rewrite these sentences. Find another way to say each sentence using the words given.**

1. Today, people ride bicycles less often than before. (used to)
   People used to ride bicycles more often than they do today.   OR
   In the past, people used to ride bicycles more often than today.

2. If I stop eating rich food, I may be able to lose weight. (diet)
   _____

3. In the future, not many people will use cash to buy things. (few)
   _____

4. If I get a better job, I can buy an apartment. (be able to)
   _____

5. There's going to be a big new mall downtown next year. (will)
   _____

10 **Write three paragraphs about yourself. In the first paragraph, describe something about your past. In the second paragraph, write about your life now. In the third paragraph, write about your future.**

I used to live in a very quiet place. . . .

Now, I live in a big city. My job is . . . . If my English improves,
I may be able to get a job with an international company. . . .

Next year, I'm going to . . . . I might. . . .

_____
_____
_____
_____
_____
_____
_____
_____
_____
_____

10 I hate working on weekends!

1 Choose the correct responses.

1. A: I enjoy working in sales.

   B: _____

   • Well, I can.   • Neither do I.   • So do I.

2. A: I like working the night shift.

   B: _____

   • Gee, I don't.   • Neither do I.   • Neither am I.

3. A: I can't stand getting to work late.

   B: _____

   • I can't.   • Neither can I.   • Well, I do.

4. A: I'm interested in using my language skills.

   B: _____

   • So am I.   • Oh, I don't.   • Oh, I don't mind.

2 Complete the sentences with the words and phrases in the box. Use gerunds.

☐ commute   ☐ start her own business   ☑ work under pressure
☐ learn languages ☐ use a computer   ☐ work with a team

1. Teresa enjoys being a journalist. She has to write a news story by 4:00 P.M. every day, but she doesn't mind _working under pressure_ .

2. Ichiro is a novelist. He writes all his books by hand because he hates _____ .

3. Gwen usually works alone all day, but she enjoys _____ , too.

4. Ellen works for a large company, but she's interested in _____ .

5. Carlos has to use Portuguese and Japanese at work, but he's not very good at _____ .

6. Cindy has to drive to work every day, but she doesn't like _____ .

3 Rewrite these sentences. Find another way to say each sentence using the words given.

1. I'm happy to answer the phone. (mind)
   <u>I don't mind answering the phone.</u>

2. I can't make decisions quickly. (not good at)

   _____

3. I hate making mistakes. (stand)

   _____

4. I don't enjoy working alone. (with a team)

   _____

4 Complete these sentences about yourself. Use gerunds.

On the job or at school
1. I like <u>meeting people, but I'm a little shy.</u>

2. I can't stand _____

3. I don't mind _____

In my free time
4. I'm interested in _____

5. I'm not interested in _____

At parties or in social situations
6. I'm good at _____

7. I'm not very good at _____

5 Choose the correct words.

1. Sam hates waiting in line. He's a very

   _____ person.
   (impatient / disorganized / punctual)

2. You can trust Rosa. If she says she's going to do something,

   she'll do it. She's very _____ .
   (hardworking / level-headed / reliable)

3. Joe isn't good at remembering things. Last week, he missed another important

   business meeting. He's so _____ .
   (efficient / forgetful / moody)

6 Jobs on the Internet

A Read these job ads. Match the job titles in the box with the ads below.

☐ flight attendant   ☐ journalist   ☐ stockbroker   ☐ truck driver

Internet Job Board

Résumé   Career Tools   Career Advice

1 Are you hardworking? Do you enjoy using computers? Do you like learning about world news? This job is for you. Must be good at working under pressure. Some evening and weekend work.

3 No previous experience necessary, but applicant must have a special license. Successful applicant will also be punctual and reliable. Excellent position for someone who enjoys traveling.

2 Must be well organized, energetic, able to make decisions quickly, and good with numbers. Applicants must be level-headed and able to take responsibility for handling other people's money. No weekend work, but some evening work required.

4 Are you good at communicating with people and solving problems? Can you speak at least two foreign languages? Do you enjoy traveling abroad? Then this job might be for you.

B What key word(s) in each job ad helped you find the answers in part A?

1. _____   3. _____

2. _____   4. _____

C Which job would be the best for you? the worst? Number them from 1 (the best) to 4 (the worst) and give reasons. List your special experience, preferences, or personal traits.

Job	Reason
____ flight attendant	_____
____ journalist	_____
____ stockbroker	_____
____ truck driver	_____

7 *Read what these people say about themselves. Then look at the jobs in the box. Choose a job each person should do and a job each person should avoid. Write sentences using the phrases given and* **because.**

☐ accountant ☐ detective ☐ lawyer ☐ nurse ☐ salesperson
☐ carpenter ☐ factory worker ☐ marine biologist ☐ model ☐ social worker

Jim

> I enjoy helping people, but I can't stand working nights and weekends.

1. (make a good / could never) Jim would probably make a good social worker because he enjoys helping people. He could never be a nurse because he can't stand working nights and weekends.

Anita

> I really like doing things with my hands. I also enjoy working with wood. I don't enjoy working in the same place every day, and I hate being in noisy places.

2. (could / couldn't) _____

_____

Allison

> I'm really interested in meeting people, and I enjoy wearing different clothes every day. I'm not so good at organizing my time, and I can't stand computers.

3. (would make a good / would make a bad) _____

_____

Young-ho

> I'm really good at selling things. I also love helping people. But I'm not so good at solving problems.

4. (could be / wouldn't make a good) _____

_____

Kevin

> I'm good at taking care of people, and I don't mind working evenings and weekends. I don't like sitting in an office all day, and I'm not good with numbers.

5. (would make a good / wouldn't want to be) _____

_____

8 Add a or an in the correct places.

1. Jerry could never be $\overset{a}{\wedge}$ nurse or teacher because he is very short-tempered and impatient with people. On the other hand, he's efficient and reliable person. So he would make good bookkeeper or accountant.

2. Mark would make terrible lawyer or executive. He isn't good at making decisions. On the other hand, he'd make excellent actor or artist because he's very creative and funny.

9 Opposites

A Write the opposites. Use the words in the box.

☐ boring	☐ forgetful	☐ lazy	☐ outgoing
✔ disorganized	☐ impatient	☐ moody	☐ unfriendly

1. efficient / _disorganized_
2. friendly / _____
3. hardworking / _____
4. interesting / _____

5. level-headed / _____
6. patient / _____
7. quiet / _____
8. reliable / _____

B Complete the sentences with words in part A.

1. Su-yin is an _____ person. She really enjoys meeting new people.

2. Becky is very _____ . One day she's happy, and the next day she's sad.

3. I can't stand working with _____ people. I like having reliable co-workers.

4. Philip is an _____ person. I'm never bored when I talk to him.

10 Crossword puzzle: Jobs

Use these words to complete the crossword puzzle.

☐ creative	☐ efficient	☐ impatient	☐ reliable	☐ tempered
☐ critical	☐ forgetful	☐ level	☐ strange	☐ working
☑ disorganized	☐ generous	☐ punctual	☐ strict	

Across

1 Amy should not be a librarian because she's very _____ . She can never find the information she needs.

5 I always do my job well. My boss never has to worry because I'm _____ .

6 Ed would make a great nurse because he's so _____-headed. He never gets anxious or upset when things go wrong.

7 Jack writes great children's stories. He's very _____ and is always thinking of new ideas.

11 A good lawyer has to remember facts. Jerry is a terrible lawyer because he's very _____ .

12 My favorite teacher at school was Mrs. Matthews. She was pretty _____ , so no one misbehaved in her class.

13 Laura is very hard-_____ . She works ten hours a day, six days a week.

Down

2 Being a limousine driver isn't a good job for Dawn. She's too _____ . She can't stand waiting for people at the airport.

3 My boss is very _____ . She gave me a big holiday bonus.

4 Sam is very short-_____ and moody. He sometimes gets angry during meetings.

8 June's assistant is very _____ . She types twice as fast as most assistants, and she never wastes time.

9 I can't stand my boss. He complains about everything I do. He's so _____ .

10 Larry arrives on time every day, even when there's traffic. He's a very _____ person.

12 Martha is very _____ . She does odd things. She often gets up in the middle of the night and writes all her reports.

11 It's really worth seeing!

1
Complete these sentences. Use the passive form of the verbs in the box.

☐ compose ☐ discover ☐ paint
☑ design ☐ invent ☐ write

1. The National Museum of the Republic in Brazil
   _____was designed_____ by the architect
   Oscar Niemeyer.

2. The play *Romeo and Juliet* _____
   by William Shakespeare in the 1590s.

3. The microwave oven _____ by
   Percy Spencer in 1947.

4. The picture *Sunflowers* _____ by
   Vincent van Gogh in 1888.

5. In 1960, a 1,000-year-old Viking settlement
   _____ in eastern Canada by
   Norwegian explorer Helge Ingstad.

6. The music for the Disney movie *The Lion King*
   _____ by Sir Elton John in 1994.

National Museum of the Republic, Brazil

2
Change these active sentences into the passive.

1. Scientists first identified the virus called HIV in 1983.
   The virus called HIV was first identified by scientists in 1983.

2. Kathryn Bigelow directed the award-winning film *The Hurt Locker* in 2008.
   _____

3. The Soviet Union launched the first satellite into space in 1957.
   _____

4. E. B. White wrote the children's novel *Charlotte's Web*.
   _____

5. Frank Lloyd Wright designed the Guggenheim Museum in New York City.
   _____

61

3 Write sentences. Use the passive.

4. Canberra, Australia
planner: Walter Burley Griffin
date: 1913

1. Angkor Wat
builder: Suryavarman II
date: about 1150

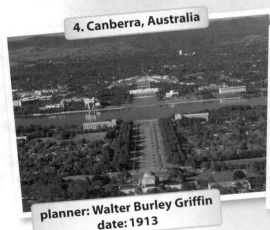
2. the Blue Mosque
designer: Mehmet Aga
date: 1616

3. Buckingham Palace
builder: the Duke of Buckingham
date: 1705

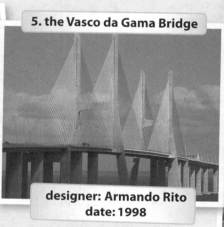
5. the Vasco da Gama Bridge
designer: Armando Rito
date: 1998

6. the Burj Khalifa
builders: 12,000 workers
date: 2010

1. Angkor Wat was built by Suryavarman II in about 1150.

2. _____

3. _____

4. _____

5. _____

6. _____

Which city?

A Read about these cities. Match the cities in the box with the correct descriptions below.

☐ Buenos Aires, Argentina   ☐ Mexico City, Mexico   ☐ Rome, Italy
☐ Manila, the Philippines   ☐ Ottawa, Canada   ☐ Timbuktu, Mali

_____ According to legend, this city was founded in 753 B.C.E. by Romulus and was named after him. However, it is more likely that the name comes from *Ruma*, the old name for the Tiber River.

_____ This city was founded by the Spanish on an island in a lake. Both the country and the city are named after an older name for the city, *Metz-xih-co*, which means "in the center of the waters of the moon."

_____ The name of this city means "fair winds" because its climate is very pleasant. It was founded twice by the Spanish – in 1536 and 1580. Five years after the city's first foundation, it was burned by local people.

_____ In the eleventh century, a village was founded in North Africa. An old woman called *Buktu* was often asked to guard the village when the villagers went hunting. The village became known as *Tim-Buktu*, the place of Buktu.

_____ Founded in 1571, this city takes its name from Tagalog, a language that is widely spoken there. It means "a place where the plant indigo is found" (*may* = "there is"; *nila* = "indigo").

_____ This city became the capital of the country in the middle of the nineteenth century. Its name is taken from the word *Adawa* in the Algonquin language, which probably means "to trade."

B Check (✓) True or False. For statements that are false, write the correct information.

	True	False
1. Both Rome and Timbuktu were named after a person.	☐	☐
2. Manila was named after a product that was found there.	☐	☐
3. Ottawa was named after the activities of the Native Americans in that region.	☐	☐
4. Buenos Aires and Mexico City were given names about their climates.	☐	☐

5 Add **is** or **are** where necessary.

Ecuador ^is situated on the equator in the northwest of South America. It made up of a coastal plain in the west and a tropical rain forest in the east. These two areas separated by the Andes mountains in the center of the country.

The economy based on oil and agricultural products. More oil produced in Ecuador than any other South American country except Venezuela. Bananas, coffee, and cocoa grown there. Many of these products exported. Hardwood also produced and exported.

Many people are of Incan origin. Several native languages spoken there, such as Quechua. Spanish spoken in Ecuador, too.

6 Complete the sentences. Use the words in the box.

☑ agricultural   ☐ electronics   ☐ peso   ☐ wheat
☐ beef   ☐ mining   ☐ tourism

1. France exports _____agricultural_____ products such as milk, butter, and cheese.

2. The _____ is the currency that is used in Chile.

3. Millions of people visit Italy every year. _____ is a very important industry there.

4. A lot of meat, especially _____ , is exported by Argentina.

5. Gold _____ is an important industry in South Africa.

6. Much of the world's _____ is grown in the Canadian prairies. It's used to make foods like bread and pasta.

7. A lot of computers and microchips are exported by Taiwan. In fact, the _____ industry is an important part of many East Asian economies.

7

Complete this paragraph with is or are and the past participle of the verbs in the box. Some words may be used more than once.

border	divide	find	locate
call	fill	know	visit

Every year, millions of tourists visit California. California _____ for its beautiful scenery, warm climate, and excellent food. There are many national parks in California. They _____ by over 30 million people every year. Many world-famous museums _____ there, including the Getty Center in Los Angeles and the San Francisco Museum of Modern Art.

The state _____ into two parts, called Northern California and Southern California. San Francisco and Yosemite National Park _____ in Northern California.

San Francisco _____ by water on three sides and is a city with a beautiful bay and several bridges. Its streets _____ always _____ with tourists. On the north end of the bay is the world-famous Napa Valley. South of San Francisco, there is an area that is famous for its computer industries; it _____ Silicon Valley. Many computer industries _____ there. Los Angeles, Hollywood, and Disneyland _____ in Southern California. Southern California _____ for its desert areas, which are sometimes next to snowcapped mountains.

8

Rewrite these sentences. Find another way to say each sentence using the words given.

1. The designer of the Montjuic Tower in Barcelona was Santiago Calatrava. (designed)

   _____

2. Switzerland has four official languages. (spoken)

   _____

3. In South Korea, a lot of people work in the automobile industry. (employed)

   _____

4. Malaysia has a prime minister. (governed)

   _____

It's really worth seeing! ▪ 65

9 Wh-questions and indirect questions

A Look at the answers. Write Wh-questions.

1. What _____

   The telephone was invented by Alexander Graham Bell.

2. Where _____

   Acapulco is located in southern Mexico.

3. When _____

   Santiago, Chile, was founded in 1541.

4. What _____

   Rice is grown in Thailand.

B Look at the answers. Write indirect questions.

1. Do you know _____

   The Golden Gate Bridge is located in San Francisco.

2. Can you tell me _____

   Don Quixote was written by Miguel de Cervantes.

3. Do you know _____

   Antibiotics were first used in 1941.

4. Could you tell me _____

   The tea bag was invented by Thomas Sullivan in 1908.

10 Complete the sentences. Use the passive of the words given.

1804 The first steam locomotive _____was built_____ (build) in Britain.

1829 A speed record of 58 kph (36 mph) _____
      (establish) by a train in Britain.

1863 The world's first underground railway _____
      (open) in London.

1964 "Bullet train" service _____ (introduce) in Japan.

1990 A speed of 512 kph (320 mph) _____ (reach) by a French high-speed train.

1995 Maglevs _____ (test) in several countries. These trains use magnets to lift
      them above the ground.

2006 The Qinghai-Tibet railway _____ (open). It is the world's highest railway and
      reaches 5,072 meters (16,640 feet).

2011 The journey time from Beijing to Shanghai _____ (reduce) from 14 hours to
      5 hours by the new maglev train.

an early steam locomotive

12 What happened?

1 *Describe what these people were doing when a fire alarm went off in their apartment building last night. Use the past continuous.*

1 Mr. Yuen
2 Andrew
3 the Hardings
4 Liliana and Eduardo
5 Jenny
6 Angela

1. <u>Mr. Yuen was cooking dinner when the fire alarm went off.</u>

2. _____

3. _____

4. _____

5. _____

6. _____

2 *Describe your activities yesterday. What were you doing at these times?*

At 9:00 A.M.
<u>At 9:00 a.m., I was having</u>
<u>breakfast at a coffee shop</u>
<u>with my friends.</u>

Around noon
_____
_____
_____

About 10:00 last night
_____
_____
_____

At 11:00 in the morning
_____
_____
_____

In the afternoon
_____
_____
_____

At this time yesterday
_____
_____
_____

3 **Complete the conversation with the correct word or phrase.**

Carl: How did you get your first job, Anita?

Anita: Well, I _____got_____ a summer job in a department store
            (got / was getting)

while I _____ at the university.
            (studied / was studying)

Carl: No, I mean your first full-time job.

Anita: But that *is* how I got my first full-time job. I _____ during the
                                                            (worked / was working)

summer when the manager _____ me a job after graduation.
                                    (offered / was offering)

Carl: Wow! That was lucky. Did you like the job?

Anita: Well, I did at first, but then things changed. I _____ the same
                                                            (did / was doing)

thing every day, and they _____ me any new responsibilities.
                                    (didn't give / weren't giving)

I _____ really bored when another company
      (got / was getting)

_____ me to work for them.
      (asked / was asking)

4 **Look at the pictures and complete these sentences.**

1. I was having a great date with my boyfriend
   when _he asked me to marry him!_____

2. I met a really nice guy last week while
   _____

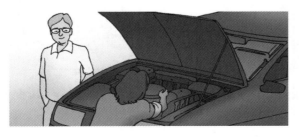

3. My car was giving me a lot of trouble, so
   _____

4. Dinner arrived while
   _____

A Scan the article. Why is Richard Branson famous?

Richard Branson

Have you ever flown on Virgin Atlantic Airways or used a Virgin Mobile cell phone? Have you booked your place in space with Virgin Galactic? If so, you have put a few more dollars in Richard Branson's pocket.

Born in Britain in 1950, Richard Branson is a world-famous businessman, entrepreneur, adventurer, and billionaire. He's best known for his charismatic personality. He's flamboyant, exciting, and personable – and he's never been afraid to take a risk.

Branson didn't have an ordinary teenage life, however. His dyslexia, or difficulty with reading and writing, made school a constant struggle. Despite this challenge, he started a national magazine called *Student* when he was only 16 years old. At 17, he decided to set up a student advisory center to help other young people.

Branson started the now-famous Virgin brand in the music industry in 1970. He began by opening a mail-order company that sold records at discount prices. Two years later, he built a recording studio and took chances on new musicians that no other recording companies would sign. In 1992, Branson sold Virgin Records for $1 billion. By then, he had moved into many other industries, including publishing, beverages, and air travel. Today, the Virgin Group comprises about 200 companies in 30 countries and employs about 50,000 people.

Virgin Atlantic Airways, which Branson started in 1984, has long been Britain's second-largest international airline. However, Branson has always dreamed about flying even higher. In 2004, he founded a space tourism company called Virgin Galactic. Anyone with $200,000 to spare can go online and book a ticket to travel in space in the future.

Even when Branson isn't working, he enjoys flying high – and breaking records. In 1991, he broke the world speed record for traveling in a hot air balloon from Japan to Canada. Seven years later, he attempted to be first to circle the world in a balloon nonstop. But bad weather forced his team to stop, and they landed near Hawaii. In his typically positive way, Branson said, "The important thing is that, in the last seven days, we've just had the greatest adventure of our lifetimes." Branson certainly knows how to enjoy life to its fullest.

B Read the article and check (✓) True or False. For statements that are false, write the correct information.

	True	False
1. Richard Branson is a very quiet person.	☐	☐
2. He took risks recording unknown musicians.	☐	☐
3. He is a pilot for Virgin Atlantic Airways.	☐	☐
4. You can now travel in space with Virgin Galactic.	☐	☐
5. He didn't break the record for going around the world in a balloon.	☐	☐

6 How long has it been?

A Write sentences. Use the present perfect continuous and *for* or *since*.

> ### Grammar note: *for* and *since*
>
> **Use *for* to describe a period of time.**
> Linda has been living in Seattle **for three months.**
> I haven't been jogging **for very long.**
> **Use *since* to describe a point of time in the past.**
> Linda has been living in Seattle **since she changed jobs.**
> I haven't been jogging **since I hurt my foot.**

1. Mia / work / model / three years

   Mia has been working as a model for three years.

2. Ruth and Peter / go / graduate school / August

   _____

3. Jim / study / Chinese / a year

   _____

4. Maria / not teach / she had a baby

   _____

5. Cindy / not live / Los Angeles / very long

   _____

6. Felix and Anna / travel / South America / six weeks

   _____

B Write sentences about yourself. Use the phrases and clauses in the box (or your own information), and *for* or *since*.

18 months	a few weeks
2006	I was in high school
ages	this morning

1. I haven't been swimming for ages.

2. _____

3. _____

4. _____

5. _____

6. _____

7 Look at the answers. Write the questions.

Chris: _What have you been doing lately?_

Alex: I've been working a lot and trying to stay in shape.

Chris: _____

Alex: No, I haven't been jogging. I've been playing tennis in the evenings with friends.

Chris: Really? _____

Alex: No, I've been losing most of the games. But it's fun. How about you? _____

Chris: No, I haven't been getting any exercise. I've been working long hours every day.

Alex: _____

Chris: Yes, I've even been working on weekends. I've been working Saturday mornings.

Alex: Well, why don't we play a game of tennis on Saturday afternoon? It's great exercise!

8 Choose the correct responses.

1. A: When I was a kid, I lived on a farm.

   B: _____
   - Really? Tell me more.
   - Oh, have you?
   - So have I.

2. A: I haven't been ice-skating for ages.

   B: _____
   - Why were you?
   - Wow! I have, too.
   - Neither have I.

3. A: I was a teenager when I got my first job.

   B: _____
   - Really? Where do you work?
   - Really? That's interesting.
   - For five years.

4. A: I haven't seen you for a long time.

   B: _____
   - I didn't know that.
   - Not since we graduated.
   - Hmm, I have no idea.

9 **Complete the answers to the questions. Use the past continuous or the present perfect continuous of the verbs given.**

1. A: Have you been working here for long?

   B: No, I <u>haven't been working</u> (work) here for very long –
   only since January.

2. A: Were you living in Europe before you moved here?

   B: No, I _____ (live) in South Korea.

3. A: How long have you been studying English?

   B: I _____ (study) it for about a year.

4. A: What were you doing before you went back to school?

   B: I _____ (sell) real estate.

5. A: What have you been doing since I last saw you?

   B: I _____ (travel) around the country.

10 **Rewrite these sentences. Find another way to say each sentence using the words given.**

1. I was getting dressed when my date
   arrived. (while)
   <u>While I was getting dressed, my date arrived.</u>

2. Todd was about 15 when he started saving up
   for a world trip. (teenager)
   _____
   _____

3. I've been a fan of that TV show since I was
   a kid. (a long time)
   _____
   _____

4. I've had a part-time job for a year. (last year)
   _____
   _____

5. I've been spending too much money lately.
   (not save enough)
   _____
   _____

6. I haven't seen you for a long time. (ages)
   _____
   _____

13 Good book, terrible movie!

1 *Choose the correct words to complete these movie reviews.*

TODAY'S Movie Reviews

The Apocalypse

This adventure movie is bizarre. The first five minutes have ___amazing___ special effects.
(amazed / amazing)
But then I was _____ because
(annoyed / annoying)
the music was very loud. I couldn't hear what the actors were saying. It was really

_____ just to sit there and not
(bored / boring)
understand the story.

The King's Speech

This drama is based on a _____
(fascinated / fascinating)
true story. King George VI had a problem making speeches, so he hired a speech therapist. Maybe it doesn't sound

_____ , but it's a must-see.
(interested / interesting)
The film has great acting and a hilarious script.
And I'm sure you'll be as _____
(excited / exciting)
by the ending as I was.

2 *Choose the correct words*

1. The latest *Pirates of the Caribbean* movie was

   ___marvelous___ (absurd / disgusting / marvelous),

   and I'd love to see it again.

2. I really enjoyed all of the *X-Men* movies. In fact, I think

   they're _____ (terrible / terrific / boring).

3. The special effects were great in *Avatar*.

   They can do such _____

   (dreadful / dumb / fantastic) things with

   3-D technology these days.

4. Christian Bale was _____

   (horrible / ridiculous / outstanding)

   in *The Dark Knight Rises*. I think he's a really

   great actor.

3 Choose the correct responses.

1. A: I think that Keira Knightly is very pretty.

   B: <u>Oh, I do, too.</u>
   - Oh, I do, too.
   - I don't like her either.

2. A: His new movie is the dumbest movie I've ever seen.

   B: _____
   - Yeah, I liked it, too.
   - I didn't like it either.

3. A: It's weird that they don't show more classic movies on TV. I really like them.

   B: _____
   - I know. It's really wonderful.
   - I know. It's strange.

4. A: I think Morgan Freeman is a fabulous actor.

   B: _____
   - Yeah, he's horrible.
   - Yeah, he's excellent.

5. A: The movie we saw last night was ridiculous.

   B: _____
   - Yes, I agree. It was exciting.
   - Well, I thought it was pretty good.

4 Write two sentences for each of these categories.

1. Things you think are exciting

   <u>I think paragliding is exciting.</u>

   _____

2. Things you are interested in

   _____

   _____

3. Things you think are boring

   _____

   _____

4. Things you are disgusted by

   _____

   _____

Classics on video

A Read about these movies available online. Match each movie type with the correct title.

_____ horror   _____ romance   _____ musical   _____ science fiction

Movie Classics

A scene from the movie *The Phantom of the Opera*

A scene from the movie *2001: A Space Odyssey*

1 The Phantom of the Opera (1925)
This is a movie that keeps you glued to your seat! It's the story of a masked composer who haunts the Paris Opera House. This silent film stars Lon Chaney as the Phantom.

2 The Wizard of Oz (1939)
For the child in all of us. Watch Dorothy's adventures in the Land of Oz. Meet the Scarecrow, the Tin Man, and the Cowardly Lion. The film stars Judy Garland. She sings some of the greatest songs in movie history. This movie is out of this world!

3 2001: A Space Odyssey (1968)
Directed by Stanley Kubrick, this is a story about two astronauts who are on a fatal mission in outer space. But it's the ship's computer, HAL, who really steals the show.

4 The African Queen (1951)
One of the greatest love stories of all time stars Katharine Hepburn and Humphrey Bogart. Hepburn is very cool to Bogart through most of the film, but she finally falls in love with him at the end.

B Write the name of the movie described.

1. a story about two people who fall in love: _____

2. a good movie for children to see: _____

3. a movie without talking: _____

4. a movie with an unusual "star": _____

C Match the expressions in column A with their meanings in column B.

A

1. glued to your seat
2. steals the show
3. out of this world
4. be cool to

B

a. outstanding
b. not be very interested in
c. watching very carefully
d. is the star

6 *Tell me more!*

A Rewrite these sentences. Use *who* or *which*.

1. *Star Wars* is a movie. It has been very popular for a long time.
   <u>Star Wars is a movie which has been very popular for a long time.</u>

2. *Walk the Line* is a movie. It is based on a true story about Johnny Cash.
   _____

3. Elizabeth Taylor was an actress. She won two Academy Awards.
   _____

4. Akira Kurosawa was a director. He was one of the most influential filmmakers in cinema.
   _____

5. *The Social Network* is a great movie. It won a lot of awards.
   _____

6. Jennifer Lopez is an actress, a dancer, and a singer. She's also a judge on a TV talent show.
   _____

B Write two sentences like those in part A about movies and entertainers. Use *who* or *which*.

1. _____
2. _____

7 *Complete the sentences. Use* that *for things or* who *for people.*

Karen: Who is Mark Twain?

Pedro: Oh, you know him. He's an author ___who___
wrote a lot of novels about life in America in the 1800s.

Karen: Oh, I remember. He wrote several stories _____
people have to read in literature classes, right?

Pedro: Yes, but people love reading them for pleasure, too.

Karen: What's his most popular book?

Pedro: I guess *Adventures of Huckleberry Finn* is the one
_____ is most famous. It's a work _____
has been very popular since it was published in the 1880s.

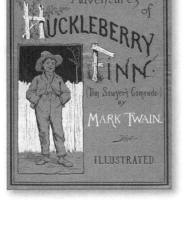

Karen: Ah, yes, I think I've heard of it. What's it about?

Pedro: It's about a boy _____ has lots of adventures with his friend Tom Sawyer. It was
one of the first American novels _____ was written in the first person. It's Huck Finn
himself _____ tells the story.

Karen: Now, that's a story _____ I'd like to read.

8 *Different kinds of movies*

A Write definitions for these different kinds of movies.
Use relative clauses and the phrases in the box.

☐ has a love story
☑ has cowboys in it
☐ has lots of excitement
☐ has singing and dancing
☐ is scary
☐ makes you laugh
☐ shows real events

1. A western is a movie that has cowboys in it.

2. A romance _____

3. A comedy _____

4. An action film _____

5. A horror film _____

6. A musical _____

7. A documentary _____

B What kind of movie in part A is your favorite? your least favorite?
Write one paragraph about each and give reasons for your opinions.

My Favorite Kind of Movie

   I really like action movies. They are movies that make me forget about all
my problems. . . .

_____

_____

_____

_____

My Least Favorite Kind of Movie

   I don't like horror movies because I think they are really dumb. Usually,
the story has characters who are not very scary. . . .

_____

_____

_____

_____

9 *Complete these sentences. Use the words in the box.*

☐ character   ☐ composer
☐ cinematography   ☐ special effects

1. I thought the _____ in the *Iron Man* movies were cool. It's incredible what they can do with computers.

2. Have you ever seen the 1965 film *Doctor Zhivago*? The _____ is beautiful, especially the lighting.

3. Hermione Granger is my favorite _____ in the Harry Potter books.

4. I've forgotten the name of the _____ who wrote *Rhapsody in Blue*. Was it George Gershwin?

10 *Rewrite this movie review. Where possible, join sentences with* who, that, *or* which.

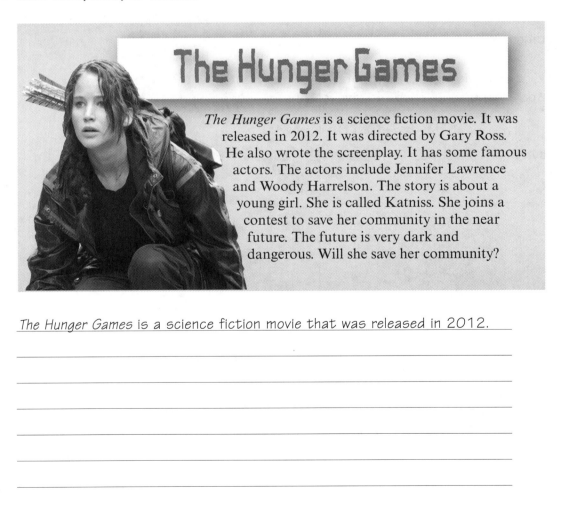

The Hunger Games

The Hunger Games is a science fiction movie. It was released in 2012. It was directed by Gary Ross. He also wrote the screenplay. It has some famous actors. The actors include Jennifer Lawrence and Woody Harrelson. The story is about a young girl. She is called Katniss. She joins a contest to save her community in the near future. The future is very dark and dangerous. Will she save her community?

The Hunger Games is a science fiction movie that was released in 2012.

_____

_____

_____

_____

_____

 # So that's what it means!

1 *What does that mean?*

A What do these gestures mean? Match the phrases in the box with the gestures.

> a. Stop!
> b. I want to turn.
> c. We need a taxi.
> d. We need help.
> e. I'm angry!

1. *e*
2. ___
3. ___
4. ___
5. ___

B Write a sentence about each situation in part A using these phrases:

> It could mean . . . It might mean . . . It must mean . . .
> Maybe it means . . . Perhaps it means . . . It probably means . . .

1. It must mean he's angry.
2. _____
3. _____
4. _____
5. _____

2 Complete the sentences. Use the correct form of the words in the box.

| ☐ annoy | ☐ confuse | ☐ embarrass | ☑ frustrate |
| ☐ bore | ☐ disgust | ☐ exhaust | |

1. I got stuck behind a really slow bus on a narrow mountain road. I felt __frustrated__ because I couldn't pass it.

2. That sign is really _____ . What does it mean? It's not clear at all.

3. The food in that restaurant on the highway is _____ . I'll never eat there again!

4. I drove for eight hours on a straight, flat road where the scenery never changed. I've never been so _____ !

5. I couldn't get into the parking space, and everyone was looking at me. It was pretty _____ .

6. I went bicycling all day. Now I'm so _____ that I'm going to sleep for 12 hours!

7. I asked the taxi driver to turn off his radio because the loud music was very _____ .

3 What would you say in each situation? Use the sentences in the box.

| ☐ Come here. | ☐ Shh. Be quiet! | ☐ That sounds crazy! | ☐ Where's the restroom? |

1. Your friend wants to dye his hair green and wear orange contact lenses.

_____

2. You can't concentrate on the movie because the people in front of you are talking.

_____

3. You wave to your friend because you want to show her something interesting.

_____

4. You just ordered a meal and want to wash your hands before you eat.

_____

A Match the proverbs with their meanings.

PROVERBS

❝

1. Don't look a gift horse in the mouth. **4.** There are plenty of fish in the sea.

2. Easier said than done. **5.** If at first you don't succeed, try, try, again.

3. An apple a day keeps the doctor away. **6.** The proof of the pudding is in the eating.

❞

MEANINGS

__3__ If you eat the right food, you will be healthy.

_____ If someone gives you a present, you should enjoy it and not ask questions or complain about it.

_____ Don't worry if you love someone who doesn't return your love. You can always find someone else.

_____ You can't be sure about something until you try it.

_____ Practice makes perfect, so you shouldn't stop trying. The harder you try, the more you'll be able to get what you want.

_____ It's harder to do something than to talk about it.

B What would you say? Choose a proverb for each situation.

1. A: Oh, yuck. Those fried brains look disgusting.

   B: Try them. They're delicious.

   A: Really? Oh, they *are* good. I'm surprised!

   B: See? _____

2. A: Hey, what happened? You look so sad.

   B: You know that guy I was dating? Well, he said he didn't want

   to see me anymore.

   A: Don't worry. You'll find someone else. _____

   _____

   B: Thanks a lot. That really helps!

3. A: You know, the person who sits next to me in class gave me these flowers for

   my birthday. It was nice of him, but they're awkward to carry around. Why didn't

   he give them to me at the end of the day instead?

   B: _____

   Just say thank you and don't complain.

4. A: You know what? I just failed my driving test! I don't think I'll bother to take it again.

   B: _____ You may pass next time!

5 *What do you think these proverbs mean?*

1. Don't cry over spilled milk.

   It could mean _____

2. Don't judge a book by its cover.

   Maybe it means _____

3. There's no such thing as a free lunch.

   It might mean _____

4. Bad news travels fast.

   It probably means _____

6 *Complete the conversation. Use each phrase in the box only once.*

Teacher: OK, class. This afternoon, we're going to take the school bus to the science museum.

Student 1: Great! I'm going to take some photos.

Teacher: I'm afraid <u>you're not allowed to</u> take photos.

Student 1: But how can they stop me? I'll use my cell phone, not a camera.

Teacher: _____ check all your things with security.

Student 2: Can I take my jacket into the museum?

Teacher: I'm not sure. _____ best to leave it on the bus.

Student 2: But what about my wallet? It might not be safe on the bus.

Teacher: Oh, _____ a good idea to keep your money with you. Keep it in your pocket.

Student 3: And what about touching things in the museum?

Teacher: There are "Don't touch!" signs next to some of the things. But _____ touch things if there is no sign.

> ☐ it might be
> ☐ it's definitely
> ☐ you can
> ☐ you have to
> ☑ you're not allowed to

Complete the conversations between a driving instructor and his student.
Use each word or phrase in the box only once.

☐ are allowed to	☐ can	☐ don't have to
☑ aren't allowed to	☐ can't	☐ have to

1. Student: This is great!

    Instructor: Hey, slow down! You _aren't allowed to_ go above the speed limit.

2. Student: Uh, what does that sign mean?

    Instructor: It means you _____ turn left.

3. Instructor: You look confused.

    Student: What . . . what does that sign mean?

    Instructor: You _____ turn left or you _____ go straight.

4. Instructor: Why are you stopping?

    Student: The sign says to stop.

    Instructor: Actually, you _____ stop. Just be prepared to, if necessary.

5. Instructor: Hey, stop! Didn't you see that sign? It means you _____ come to a complete stop.

    Student: What sign? I didn't see any sign.

2

3

4

5

8 Rewrite these sentences. Find another way to say each sentence using the words given.

1. Maybe it means you're not allowed to fish here. (may)
   It may mean you're not allowed to fish here.

2. You can't light a fire here. (allowed)
   _____

3. Perhaps that sign means you're not allowed to swim here. (might)
   _____

4. I think that sign means you can get food here. (probably)
   _____

5. You need to be quiet after 10:00 P.M. (have got to)
   _____

9 Complete each conversation using the words in the box.

☐ confusing   ☐ embarrassing   ☐ exhausting   ☐ impatient   ☐ irritating

1. A: I fell asleep during class this afternoon. The teacher had to wake me up.
   B: Oh, that's _____ !

2. A: I went to the movies last night. The couple who sat behind me talked during the entire movie.
   B: That's _____ !

3. A: I drove all night to get there on time.
   B: Oh, that's _____ ! How can you keep your eyes open?

4. A: Did Anna give you directions to the party?
   B: She did, but they're really _____ . Hey, can I get a ride with you?

5. A: This movie is taking forever to download. Why does it have to take so long?
   B: You are so _____ ! There, look. It's done!

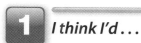

What would you do?

1 *I think I'd . . .*

A What would you do in these situations? Check (✔) an answer or write your own suggestion.

1. Your classmate leaves her new smartphone in the classroom.
   - ☐ run after her and give it back to her immediately
   - ☐ take it home overnight to try it out
   - ☐ _____

2. Someone climbs through your neighbor's window.
   - ☐ call the police
   - ☐ ring the doorbell
   - ☐ _____

3. Your boss makes things difficult for you at work.
   - ☐ talk to your boss
   - ☐ look for another job
   - ☐ _____

4. A friend sounds unhappy on the phone.
   - ☐ ask your friend if he or she has a problem
   - ☐ tell lots of jokes to make your friend laugh
   - ☐ _____

B Write about what you would do in the situations in part A. Use the phrases in the box.

> I'd . . .   I might . . .   I guess . . .
> I'd probably . . .   I think I'd . . .

1. _If my classmate left her new smartphone in the classroom, I think_
   I'd run after her and give it back to her immediately.

2. _____
   _____

3. _____
   _____

4. _____
   _____

2 *Complete these sentences with information about yourself.*

1. If a relative asked to borrow some money, I'd _____

2. If I had three wishes, _____

3. If I could have any job I wanted, _____

4. If I had a year of vacation time, _____

5. If I could change one thing about myself, _____

3 *Choose the correct word.*

1. When I went back to the parking lot, I tried to get into someone else's

   car _____ by _____ mistake.
      (by / in / with)

2. My friend _____ to cheating on the biology exam,
      (returned / confessed / said)

   but his teacher still failed him.

3. I'm in a difficult _____ at work. I don't
      (divorce / predicament / problem)

   know whether to talk to my boss about it or just quit.

4. If I saw someone _____ in a store,
      (cheating / shoplifting / shopping)

   I'd tell the store manager immediately.

5. My uncle died and left me $20,000. I'm going to _____ most of it.
      (invest / return / sell)

6. I'd go _____ to the police if I saw someone breaking
      (seriously / simply / straight)

   into a house.

7. There is so much great music to download from the Internet. I don't know

   what to _____ .
      (choose / confess / fix)

8. My aunt won't let me use her car because she thinks I'm a terrible driver.

   She has a _____ . I had two accidents last year!
      (flat tire / point / reward)

4 *What to do?*

A Read the article. Match what happened to a possible action.

What happened

1. You sat on a park bench that had wet paint on it. You ruined your clothes. There was no "Wet Paint" sign.

2. You checked your bank statement and noticed that there was a deposit of $1,000. You didn't make the deposit. You're sure it was a bank error.

3. You bought a camera on sale at a store, but it didn't work right. The salesclerk said, "We can't do anything about it."

4. You were not happy with the grade you got in an important class.

5. Your next-door neighbors borrowed your vacuum cleaner. When they returned it, it was damaged.

6. A friend gave you an expensive vase for your birthday, but you didn't really like it.

Possible actions

☐ I guess I'd take it back to the store and exchange it for something else.

☐ I guess I'd write a letter of complaint to the manufacturer.

☐ Maybe I'd ask them to repair it.

☐ I think I'd make an appointment to see the instructor to talk about it.

☐ I'd probably wait until the next month to see if the mistake is corrected.

☐ I'd write a letter to the city council and ask them to pay for the damage.

B What would you do in each situation? Write another possible action.

1. _____

2. _____

3. _____

4. _____

5. _____

6. _____

5 *What would you have done in these situations? Use* **would have** *or* **wouldn't have.**

1. Diana had dinner in a restaurant and then realized she
didn't have any money. She offered to wash the dishes.
<u>I wouldn't have washed the dishes. I would have called</u>
<u>a friend to bring me some money.</u>

2. John was on a bus when the woman next to him started talking
loudly on a cell phone. He asked her to speak more quietly.
_____
_____

3. Bill invited two friends to dinner on Friday, but they came on
Thursday by mistake. He told them to come back the next day.
_____
_____

4. Bob's neighbors had their TV on very loud late at night.
Bob called and complained to the police.
_____
_____

5. Ellen had a houseguest who was supposed to stay for
three days, but the woman was still there three weeks
later. Ellen finally gave her a bill for her room and board.
_____
_____

6. Susan accidentally broke a glass at a friend's house.
She decided not to say anything about it.
_____
_____

6 *Write two things you should have done or shouldn't have done last week,*
last month, and last year.

1. Last week: <u>Last week, I should have . . .</u>
_____

2. Last month: _____
_____

3. Last year: _____

7 Advice column

A Complete each letter with the correct forms of the verbs in each box.

☐ borrow ☐ disagree ☑ marry ☐ spend
☐ deny ☐ enjoy ☐ save ☐ worry

Ask Harriet

Dear Harriet,

I've never written to an advice columnist before, but I have a big problem. I'm going out with this really nice guy. He's very sweet to me, and I really want to _____marry_____ him. In fact, we plan to have our wedding next summer. But he has a problem with money. He _____ money like crazy! Sometimes he _____ money from me, but he never pays it back. I want to _____ money because I want us to buy an apartment when we get married. However, if I tell him he has a problem with money, he _____ it. He says, "I _____ with you. You _____ too much. You never want to go out and _____ yourself." What can I do?   –J. M., Seattle

☐ accept ☐ admit ☑ agree ☐ find ☐ forget ☐ refuse

Dear J. M.,

You and your boyfriend must _____agree_____ on how you spend your money *before* you get married. If you both _____ that there is a problem, you could probably _____ an answer. He should _____ your idea of saving some money. And you shouldn't always _____ to go out and have fun. Don't _____ that talking can really help. Good luck!

—Harriet

B What advice would you give J. M.? Write a reply to her letter.

_____

_____

_____

_____

_____

8 | *To accept or to refuse?*

A Complete the conversation with *would* or *should* and the correct tense of the verbs given.

Lacey: Guess what, Tina! A university in New Zealand has offered me a scholarship.

Tina: Great! When are you going?

Lacey: That's just it. I may not go. What ___would___ you ___do___ (do) if your boyfriend asked you not to go?

Tina: Well, I _____ (try) to convince him that it's a good opportunity for me.

Lacey: I've tried that. He said I could study the same thing here.

Tina: If I were you, I _____ (talk) to him again. You know, I once missed a big opportunity.

Lacey: Oh? What happened?

Tina: I was offered a job in Los Angeles, but my husband disliked the idea of moving, so we didn't go. I _____ (take) the job. I've always regretted my decision. In my situation, what _____ you _____ (do)?

Lacey: Oh, I _____ (accept) the offer.

Tina: Well, there's the answer to your predicament. Accept the scholarship!

B What would you do if you were Lacey? Why?

If I were Lacey, . . . _____

_____

9 | *What would you do if you found a magic lamp? Complete these sentences.*

1. I would hide it and come back for it later. _____

2. I wouldn't _____

3. I could _____

4. I might _____

5. I might not _____

What's your excuse?

1 *People are making a lot of requests of James. Write the requests.*
Use ask, tell, *or* say *and reported speech.*

James Kelly

1. William: "James, take my phone calls."
2. Jenny: "Can you do an Internet search for me, James?"
3. Dave: "Could you check this flash drive for viruses?"
4. Anita: "James, put this information on a spreadsheet."
5. Linda: "Don't forget to add paper to the copier, James."
6. Ricky: "Reformat this text file as a PDF file."
7. Chuck: "Get me some coffee, James."
8. Katie: "Make five copies of the agenda before the meeting."
9. Pete: "Could you give me a ride home?"
10. Olive: "Don't be late to work again."

1. <u>William told James to take his phone calls.</u>

2. _____

3. _____

4. _____

5. _____

6. _____

7. _____

8. _____

9. _____

10. _____

2 Nouns and verbs

A Complete the chart.

Noun	Verb	Noun	Verb
acceptance	accept	_____	criticize
_____	apologize	_____	excuse
_____	complain	_____	invite
_____	compliment	_____	sympathize

B Complete these sentences. Use the correct form of the words from part A.

1. This coffee tastes awful. I'm going to ____complain____ to the waiter about it.

2. I _____ an invitation to Terry and Anna's house for dinner.

3. I didn't want to go to Cindy's party, so I made up an _____ .

4. I was rude to my teacher. I must _____ to him.

5. My English teacher said my essay was excellent. It felt really nice to
   get a _____ from a teacher.

6. My parents _____ everything I do. I wish they weren't so negative.

7. I'm sorry you have the flu. I had it last week, so I can _____ with you.

8. I received an _____ to Janet's party. I can't wait to go.

3 Choose the correct verb. Use the past tense.

☐ express   ☐ give   ☑ make   ☐ offer   ☐ tell

1. I _____made_____ a complaint to the police because our
   neighbors' party was too noisy.

2. Larry _____ an excuse for being late for
   work. He said there had been a traffic jam on the highway.

3. I couldn't go to the meeting, so I _____
   my concerns in an email.

4. Wendy told me she was graduating from college, so
   I _____ her my congratulations.

5. Jill was very funny at the class party. As usual,
   she _____ lots of jokes.

4 What a great excuse!

A Match the invitations with the excuses. Then underline the words and phrases that helped you.

Invitations

1 Can you come to the movies on Saturday night? It's a Reese Witherspoon movie, and it starts at 9:00 at City Plaza. If you're free earlier, you could meet Ursula and me at Pizza Parlor around 8:00. Also, we thought we might go to a nightclub after the film. Hope you can make it!

2 Would you like to come to our barbecue on Sunday? It's going to start around noon. In case you've forgotten, we live at 2135 Main Street. We're going to have kebabs and BBQ chicken, but there will also be vegetarian food. You're a vegetarian, aren't you? Let me know.

3 Hi! Nicola and I are going hiking on Saturday or Sunday. We thought we'd start early and hike the Forest Hill trail. Nicola said to bring some food and plenty of water. Oh, and Phil might be joining us. If you can't make it, you'd better have a good excuse!

Excuses

a Thanks for your invitation. Unfortunately, I won't be able to make it. I have to work in the afternoon. I must say I'm really annoyed with my boss. She lives for her work and expects me to do the same. Anyway, enjoy yourselves!

b I got your email – thanks. I'd love to come, but I'll be out of town all weekend. I'm going hiking, too. I hope you have a great time and that the weather is good.

c Thanks for your email. I'm afraid I'm busy in the evening. It's my dad's 50th birthday, and I'm taking him and Mom out to dinner. But I might be able to come dancing later. Let's keep it open – OK?

B Read the excuses again. Who is going to do these things? Write *a*, *b*, or *c*.

_____ be outdoors all weekend

_____ go out on the weekend

_____ work on the weekend

5 | *Sorry, but . . .*

A The teacher wants to have a class picnic on Saturday. Look at the excuses that students gave her. Change each excuse into reported speech using *say*.

1. John: "I'm getting my hair cut."

    John said he was getting his hair cut.

2. Maria: "My sister is having a baby shower."

3. Jim: "I may have some houseguests on Saturday."

4. Keiko and Rie: "We're going camping this weekend."

5. Carlos: "I'm sorry, but I'll be busy on Saturday afternoon."

B Change these excuses into reported speech using *tell*.

1. Emma: "I signed up for a scuba diving class."

    Emma told her she had signed up for a scuba diving class.

2. Tom and Kyle: "We'll be moving to our new apartment that day."

3. Franco: "I watch the football game on TV every Saturday."

4. Juliet: "I've already made plans to do something else."

C Write excuses for three more students. Use your own ideas.

1.

2.

3.

6 What did they say?

A Match the reports of what people said in column A with the descriptions in column B.

A	B
1. Charlie said he was really worried about Tina. She seemed very depressed. __c__	a. giving a compliment
2. William told me he was sorry to hear about my sick grandmother. _____	b. offering sympathy
3. Ruth said she would be studying on Saturday night. (But she'll actually be at the movies.) _____	c. expressing a concern
4. Robert told me he couldn't come for dinner on Friday. He said he had to work late. _____	d. telling a lie
5. Ben told Linda her new blouse was very pretty. _____	e. making an excuse

B Write each person's original words.

1. Charlie: "I'm really worried about Tina. She seems very depressed."

2. William: _____

_____

3. Ruth: _____

_____

4. Robert: _____

_____

5. Ben: _____

_____

7 *Choose the correct responses.*

1. A: We're going to go horseback riding. Do you want to join us?

   B: _____

   - Sorry, I won't be able to.
   - What's up?

2. A: I'm really sorry. We'll be out of town this weekend.

   B: _____

   - I've made other plans.
   - No problem.

3. A: Meet us at 7:00. OK?

   B: _____

   - Oh, that's all right.
   - Sounds like fun.

4. A: I'm sorry. I won't be able to make it.

   B: _____

   - Well, never mind.
   - Great.

8 *Yes or no?*

A Which expressions would you use to accept an invitation? refuse an invitation?
Check (✓) the correct answer.

	Accept	Refuse		Accept	Refuse
1. I'm really sorry.	☐	✓	5. I won't be able to make it.	☐	☐
2. Great.	☐	☐	6. I'm busy.	☐	☐
3. Sounds like fun.	☐	☐	7. Thanks a lot.	☐	☐
4. I've made other plans.	☐	☐	8. I'd love to.	☐	☐

B Use the expressions in part A to accept or refuse these invitations.
Offer an excuse if you refuse.

1. Would you like to come to a soccer match with me tomorrow?

   _____

2. That new action movie looks great! Do you want to see it with me?

   _____

3. A friend asked me to go to the mall after class. Do you want to join us?

   _____